Autumn Winds

Encounters with a World in Transition

I0105522

Craig Newberger

Illustrations by Sherrie York
Photographs by Steve Morello
Appendix by Ron Smith

Grackle Publishing - Ambler, Pennsylvania

Grackle

An imprint of Grackle Publishing, LLC

gracklepublishing.com

Copyright © 2024 Craig Newberger

All rights reserved.

Library of Congress Control Number: 2024941684

ISBN: 978-1-951620-23-3

No part of this publication may be reproduced, distributed, or transmitted in any form or by any means, including photocopying, recording, or other electronic or mechanical methods, without the prior written permission of the publisher, except in the case of brief quotations embodied in critical reviews and certain other noncommercial uses permitted by copyright law. For permission requests, write to grackle@ gracklepublishing.com.

To Sherrie York, Steve Morello, and Ron Smith
For your invaluable contributions to this series
With friendship and appreciation

Autumn Winds: Encounters with a World in Transition

On the Move:

Flying Cigars (Chimney Swift) 9
Floating on the Wind (Spiders) 13
Return to the Skies (Bald Eagle) 19
The Secret Migration (American Eel) 25
Autumnal Pool Party (Marbled Salamander) 30
Nighttime Aerialists (Bats) 34
King and Queen of the Butterflies (Monarch Butterfly) 39
A Moment with a Falcon (Merlin) 45

Autumnal Palette:

Life After Labor Day (Asters and Goldenrods) 48
The Great Reveal (Fall Foliage) 52
The Last Wildflower (Witch Hazel) 56
Treasure in the Dunes (Cranberries) 60
The Fruits of November (Mushrooms) 64
Crunch Time (Oaks) 69

Prelude to Winter:

The Steward (Eastern Chipmunk) 74
Night Screamer (Red Fox) 78
Squid Pro Quo (Squid) 82
White Lightning (Northern Gannet) 86
The First Snow 91
Among the Evergreens (Conifers) 94

Appendix: Community Science by Ron Smith 98

Acknowledgments 101

Preface

The expansive sugar maple on our school campus is a testament to time and space. Every year in late October, I am drawn to the vibrant color display of this tree. Sunlight streams through the leaves, creating tints and tones of orange, red, and yellow. On the ground, surrounding the base of its trunk, lie scores of fallen leaves. I rake them into a heaping mound and invite a group of watchful kindergarten children to jump in.

Fall is a season of substantial change as plants and animals make necessary preparations for winter's challenging weather. Numerous animals are on the move, many traveling thousands of miles to reach new feeding grounds. Shorebird migration continues in fall and is joined by a host of other species, peaking in the weeks surrounding the autumnal equinox. More than four billion birds stream south during fall migration, many traveling between continents, reminding us that both breeding and wintering grounds are critical to survival.

Species of dragonflies, beetles, and butterflies also engage in seasonal movements. Both green darner dragonflies and monarch butterflies are frequently seen at hawk watching sites. Monarch butterflies, each weighing less than a gram, journey from as far north as the Canadian provinces to the temperate forests of Mexico, making a partial return in spring. Flapping and gliding on delicate wings, they can travel more than a hundred miles in a single day.

Many species of mammals head south in the fall, including three species of northeastern bats and our largest mammals, the great whales. The baleen whales, including the blue, finback, and humpback, leave the colder northern waters for warmer ones in the tropics. Squirrels, chipmunks, mice, and other rodents furtively gather and stash food for the long winter ahead, while groundhogs and brown bats, with increasing appetites, prepare for hibernation.

The opening prelude of autumn's seasonal symphony quietly points to subtle changes in the color palette. Vibrant yellow goldenrod plumes sway beneath the sun. Purple, blue, and white petaled asters grow scattered among straw-colored grasses. Along the coast, dried sea lavender flowers add pockets of color to fields of salt meadow hay. Yellow, red, and purple beach plums dot the dunes along with orange and red rosehips.

Conduits between earth and sky, deciduous trees offer a glorious display of color before sending their leaves off with the wind. The season's crescendo can be seen in the canary yellow of hickory and tulip leaves and the deep crimson of red maples. Swamps and bogs glisten as deep green tamarack needles turn gold.

Once the leaves of witch hazel have fallen to the ground, its bright yellow flowers, resembling spiders on a stick, come into full bloom. The flowers release a pleasant fragrance, attracting late season moths, flies, beetles, and bees.

In wooded areas, following a substantial rain, the fungi kingdom erupts in an eye-catching display. Triggered by the moisture seeping below the soil, the fruiting bodies grow to emerge as the mushrooms we encounter along the ground. From indigo milk caps to red and white fly agarics to orange and yellow chicken of the woods, mushrooms are the fruiting bodies of thread-like mycelial masses networking below ground. They play a vital ecological role in decomposition while adding interest, beauty, and color to the autumn landscape.

As the winter solstice nears, we attach symbolic roles to evergreens. Coniferous trees, including pines, spruces, firs, and cedars, represent everlasting life. Along with ferns and mosses on the forest floor, the conifers break through the muted tones of the winter landscape. They remind us that spring will come.

The plants and animals in this book can be found throughout the Northeastern and Midwestern portions of the United States with the obvious exception of two animals found along the coast. Each essay is based on a personal encounter. Within these pages, I wish to share my enthusiasm and encourage readers to venture outdoors and experience the natural world in transition.

Flying Cigars

Every year, during the third week of September, our local birding group offers a chimney swift watch at a Philadelphia school. Although the entire event lasts twenty minutes or so, it is worth the effort to get there. Most outdoor programs centered around birds take place in forests, fields, wetlands, and shorelines. However, this one takes place in an urban setting among timeworn school buildings. The school's weathered chimneys attract the migrating swifts, serving as the perfect evening roosts. Birders scan the skies on many early evenings, hoping for a sign that a flock might soon arrive. Once sighted, word of their chosen location races throughout the community. People with lawn chairs and binoculars gather on the school blacktop, singularly focused on bird behavior rarely seen. On one occasion, I saw hundreds of birds repeatedly circling high above a chimney for a good thirty minutes before they all disappeared. They reminded me of wind-whipped swirls of smoke drawn back down into a flue on a windy day.

Shortly before dusk, as we arrive at the school, there are rarely more than two or three chimney swifts circling above the chimney. As the sky begins to darken, groups of swifts fly into the area from every direction, creating a loosely growing, swirling mass. A few minutes past sunset, the swifts spiral to form a soaring column. Above the chimney crown, I watch several birds break away from the group, shifting side to side, wings angled and tail feathers spread, to disappear inside the chimney. Other swifts dive headfirst. When I zoom in on the entrance to the chimney, several pop out to rejoin the swirling masses. Perhaps they want to relish a bit more flight time before settling in for the night.

My binoculared companions and I are willing captives for a fascinating twenty minutes, arrival to roost. We become aware that the dusky colors of the evening sky are deepening. There are only a few stragglers left circling the roost, and as they disappear, so do the watchers. We leave gifted with the memory of a rarely noticed event in a city humming with activity.

What draws these birds to chimneys? Look at their legs. Their short legs, and large wings, prevent them from perching on tree branches like a songbird. When not in flight, they must cling to vertical surfaces, holding on with their long claws and stiff, spiny tail feathers. Historically, they roosted in caves and in the cavities of large trees found in old growth forests. When the forests were cleared to make way for farms, towns, and cities, the swifts needed to find an alternative, so began using tall chimneys in much the same way they had used trees. Chimneys provided adequate space and just the right surface for clinging.

In early fall, chimney swifts migrate to South America, a trip of some three thousand miles. Large flocks form along three main routes, the Atlantic coast, the eastern side of the Appalachian Mountains, and the Mississippi flyway. They fly across or around the Gulf of Mexico and then head south to Peru, Brazil, and other countries in the Amazon basin. Here they find a host of aerial insects that are their most important food source.

Chimney swifts spend most of their lives on the wing. Due to their compact body shape, they are often referred to as flying cigars powered by rapidly beating wings. Their narrow wings are longer than their bodies and their tails are short. Like bats, they fly at high altitudes, feasting on insects on the wing. A single swift can eat over a thousand mosquitoes in a day. When hunting, a chimney swift can fly up to 150 miles per hour, one of the fastest birds on record. The summer months offer the best chance of spotting a few individuals hunting at a time. Our suburban neighborhood hosts a few each year. If you have abundant insects, they will come.

Surprisingly, these resourceful birds even bathe in flight. They can wash in the rain as they fly or glide down to ponds and streams, dipping and bouncing off the surface and then shaking themselves dry.

Unlike songbirds, swifts do not sing a melodic song. They are constantly chattering, producing a high-pitched chirping sound like the buzzing of insects. You can hear them vocalize in flight, at rest inside a chimney, and when they feed their young.

During the summer breeding season, only a single pair takes up residence in a chimney. Although nonbreeding birds occasionally join them, you will only see large flocks of swifts during fall migration. Both parents share the tasks of nest building and raising the young and are occasionally assisted by nonbreeding birds. Using glue-like saliva from a gland underneath the tongue, the birds stick a cup-like nest of small twigs to the wall of a chimney, cave, or hollow tree. Within two weeks, the young outgrow their nest and develop the ability to cling to the chimney wall, sometimes before their eyes open.

Due to a variety of factors, the population of chimney swifts in North America has declined by sixty-seven percent since 1970, rendering them a "species of greatest concern" in several states. The factors leading to this serious decline are numerous. The felling of trees, ideal for nesting and roosting, challenged breeding pairs and placed additional stresses on the birds during migration. Eventually, fireplace chimneys, which had substituted for the trees, were altered to accommodate oil and gas furnaces and chimneys were capped and lined. Arbitrary increases in the use of pesticides and chemical applications reduce insect abundance and diversity—the very food vital to their survival. Additional threats during migration include weather, predation, human interventions, and illness. Increasingly, the chimney swift's winter habitat has been diminished or destroyed.

We can work toward increasing swift populations by reversing some of these trends. In fact, one of our neighbors built and installed a twelve-foot chimney swift tower in his backyard. "What is that thing?" I am frequently asked. I am eager to answer this question. It gives me a chance to talk about the swifts, touch on threats to their survival, and point out that this tower is one person's commitment to making a difference. Lately, I have been to several parks in our area and am noticing other chimney swift towers popping up. Some are Eagle Scout projects that inform other scouts and their families about the increasing threats to swifts, introducing the tower as an option to mitigate human impact.

In addition to constructing a tower, there are many things we can do to reverse the trend and help protect this enigmatic species. If you have a chimney, you could make sure the damper is closed during the summer months when it is not in use and refrain from capping it. In addition, we need to protect our insect populations by avoiding the use of pesticides and planting pollinator-friendly gardens.

As summer fades to fall, chimney swifts are busy preparing for their journey south. They put on extra body fat while molting and replacing their tail and wing feathers. Their final itinerary is dictated by the weather. If the air is still, the birds remain in the vicinity of a roost site for several days. When a cold front arrives, they spread their wings at the crack of dawn and ride the wind like surfers on a wave. One day, the sky is filled with swirling birds, and the next day, they are gone for the season. I look forward to this spectacle every year. Along with fields of goldenrod and hawks soaring overhead, it marks the beginning of the fall season.

Floating on the Wind

On a cool, foggy September morning, I wake to a world transformed by spiders. As far as the eye can see, tapestries of silk glisten in the morning sun. Delicate threads, woven into an ethereal latticework, are bejeweled with water droplets. What lay unseen beneath the warmth of yesterday's sun produces today's breathtaking enchantment. I settle in to enjoy it while I can. Once the sun makes its way through the fog, the work of the weavers will disappear.

Despite their diversity and beauty, spiders are among the most underappreciated animals on the planet. Long before there were dinosaurs, spiders roamed the earth. Throughout history, spiders have played a vital role in forest, field, and aquatic food webs as both predators and prey. Their abilities and adaptations rival our own. There are spiders that can jump twenty times their own body length, sail through the air on a tiny thread, and produce four or five different varieties of silk. Most spiders are harmless to humans and perform valuable ecological services by controlling insect pests and pollinating plants.

Like insects and crabs, spiders belong to the arthropod phylum, which includes a wide variety of invertebrates with jointed legs and hard protective exoskeletons. However, spiders are not insects. Insects have six legs, two antennae, wings at some stage of their lives, and three body parts composed of a head, thorax, and abdomen. Spiders have eight legs and two body parts. The head and thorax are fused together to form a cephalothorax which is attached to an abdomen. Underneath the head, spiders have small leg-like feelers, called pedipalps, covered with fine hairs that sense vibrations and assist with web spinning and feeding. Pedipalps are also employed by the males in the delivery of sperm to the females. The number, shape, and arrangement of spider eyes varies in different species according to their requirements for depth perception and motion sensing. Consider the secondary eyes of jumping spiders. The combination of their six smaller eyes and their two large eyes gives them a 360-degree view of the world, which allows them to spot available prey in any direction.

Once a spider has successfully captured its future meal, it inserts two hollow fangs called chelicerae into the body. When capturing prey or when used in defense, a spider's fangs fill with venomous fluid which it injects upon impact. The venom liquefies the victim's internal organs, allowing the spider to extract its meal in much the same way we use a straw. In most cases, the strength of its venom is lethal solely to insects and other tiny creatures. Only one type of spider in our region, the black widow, is known for its toxic bite. Despite its dangerous reputation, there have been no human fatalities recorded since 1983. Typically, a black widow spider, like all other spiders, will do just about anything to escape human interactions, including running away and hiding. However, when these strategies fail and the spider senses imminent danger, it employs its last line of defense—a bite.

There are many species of arachnids that are not spiders, including scorpions, ticks, mites, and harvestmen, commonly known as daddy-longlegs. Every fall, my students and I find harvestmen moving among the leaf litter beneath the tree canopy. "It's a spider!" Debates ensue. "No, it's not." Everyone squats to get a better look. "It's deadly poisonous!" A few students pull back. "What!?" This back and forth between future scientists demands further observation. We note our subject has eight legs like a spider. Unlike a spider's two body parts, the harvestman has one. Its singular body part consists of a fused cephalothorax and abdomen. Looking head on, the students report there are only two eyes, not the six to eight commonly found on spiders. As it moves forward, the second pair of its long, thin legs hover, then tap the ground. A bold young hand reaches out, touching one of the sensitive legs. The harvestman flees, scuttling to the nearest protective shelter. The urban myth that harvestmen have a poisonous bite has no basis in fact. They possess neither fangs nor venom sacs. They can, if disturbed, release a non-toxic, malodorous chemical from their bodies to discourage predators. If caught, they can release a leg which will twitch spasmodically, drawing the predator's attention to the leg and away from the escaping harvestman.

Spiders and harvestmen differ in meal acquisition and preference. Harvestmen are omnivores, dining on live and decaying plants as well as animals, while spiders are predators. Spiders have book lungs, while harvestmen have spiracles on their legs for respiration. All spiders can produce and spin silk, but harvestmen do not have this ability. Cellar spiders, whose lofty webs drape many a basement, resemble harvestmen with their long legs and sporadic movements. Upon closer inspection, cellar spiders have two body parts, eight legs, and multiple eyes—all characteristic of true spiders. There is one family of insects that is often confused with harvestmen. The legs of craneflies are long and thin, resembling harvestmen, but craneflies have six legs, three body parts, antennae, and wings.

Old farmhouses provide the perfect habitat for spiders. When we lived in a three-hundred-year-old stone farmhouse, we shared our front porch with several garden spiders. During the lengthening September evenings, while we were fast asleep, large black and yellow orb spiders worked the graveyard shift, constructing webs between our wooden posts and the overhang. When we opened the door in the morning and stepped outside, we found our porch decorated with intricate webs. Close examination revealed a unique zigzag "signature" woven into each web. This zigzag pattern, called a stabilimentum, helps steady the web and may also warn birds of its presence while attracting insects. A female spider will eat the central strands of her web at night, repairing it with fresh strands in the early morning hours. Often, we located the spider, head down, near the center of her web. Nearby, were multiple prey items wrapped in silk, awaiting future consumption.

For centuries, humans have marveled at the strength and elasticity of spider silk, which has a tensile strength greater than steel and a flexibility greater than nylon. A spider's agile spinnerets, located on the underside of the abdomen, combine single threads into strands of different widths and strengths. This makes it possible to use the silk strands for a wide range of purposes. Draglines are left behind when a spider travels, making it possible to retrace its steps and return to the web. They are also used for climbing trees, rocks, or the walls of buildings. Spider draglines were an inspiration in the development of mountaineering equipment. Some spiders build trap lines in the center of the web that vibrate when an insect touches or lands on the delicate threads. Once felt, the vibrations guide the spider to its victim. Spiders also use their silk to wrap and protect their egg cases, form trapdoor covers, construct winter sleeping chambers, and bind their prey.

Each species of spider produces a web that best fits its needs. Orb weaver webs contain concentric circles with large spokes that meet in the middle like a bicycle wheel. The spiders wait in their webs or hide nearby in anticipation of tangled prey. Spiders who live and hunt from the depths of a burrow, often located between plants and rocks, create funnel webs. The web appears as a hole encircled by a film of silk in which the spider resides. These funnels are designed to allow the spider to race out at a moment's notice. Sheet webs are composed of thick strands of silk that stretch between grasses and branches. The spiders wait beneath the web in anticipation of a victim. Triangle webs are woven into a shape reminiscent of a pizza slice. Unlike other webs, they are not sticky. Instead, they have a fuzzy texture to smother potential prey. The triangle weaver spider uses the web like a slingshot. It pulls a line of silk and releases it, launching the spider and web forward to trap its prey. Cobwebs are abandoned webs. We find them in our homes and outbuildings especially when we, too, have abandoned the area for a time.

Not all spiders spin webs. During night explorations, I sometimes shine my flashlight along the ground. If I am lucky, tiny, sparkly lights look back at me. These lights are the eyeshine of wolf spiders, muppet-like spiders that spend most of their time in burrows, often emerging at night. Their secondary eyes contain small membranes that act as tiny mirrors, enabling the spiders to take in as much light as possible. Once prey is detected, wolf spiders chase and capture it. The sole use of their spinnerets is to produce silk to wrap and protect their eggs. This wrapping resembles a small ball and is referred to as an egg sac.

During creek explorations, it is a treat when we find fishing spiders, large aquatic spiders that float on the surface film. They feed by ambushing their prey, including aquatic insects and small fish, and have no use for web traps. However, they can spin silken lines, or draglines, to avoid being carried downstream. These draglines can also be used by females to lay a trail of pheromone-laced threads across the water's surface to attract males.

Fall is the ideal time for seeing spiders. When the temperature cools and leaves fall to the ground, young spiderlings are ready to disperse. Energized by the sun and carried on gentle breezes, you can see them floating through the air on miniature parachutes. When ready, the spiderling climbs to a summit, perhaps a flower blossom, twig, or a grass tip, and faces the wind. It extends its eight legs and lifts its abdomen above its perch. The spinnerets shoot out jets of liquid silk that harden on contact with the air, forming threads of great strength yet light enough to float on air. When the spider lets go of its perch, it drifts much like a helium balloon. This behavior, known as ballooning, is also referred to as kiting. Ballooning is thought to distribute spiderling species in random fashion. Ballooning spiders have been found more than two miles high riding on atmospheric data balloons and a thousand miles out to sea on the sails of ships. Spiders may lack the navigation skills of human aviators, but they are not completely at the mercy of the air currents. While in flight, they can adjust their course by climbing up and down their silken threads, pulling on them, and winding them up. They can also spin additional threads with their spinnerets.

Alongside flying squirrels, gliding geckos, and flying fish, spiders are one of a small number of creatures that a have found a way to soar through the air without wings. Manufacturing their own equipment, they mastered the elements of flight long before humans arrived on the planet. By contrast, humans became aviators a little more than a century ago.

For four hundred million years, spiders have graced this planet, providing important life lessons for us. Often taking hours to build their webs, they are tenacious. Watching and waiting for an insect to arrive, they are models of patience. Traveling on a single thread, they demonstrate that astonishing endeavors can be accomplished by the tiniest creatures.

As the fog dissipates, the intricate webs once again blend into the grasses. The sun has reclaimed the day, setting in motion the process of evaporation, drying each strand. In concert with the strengthening rays of the sun, colorful patches of wildflowers light the day. I lean over to examine multiple yellow flowers on a spire of goldenrod. I pull a hand lens out of my pocket. Aided by the magnification of this tiny device, I can see small visitors within the bright yellow rays. A tiny yellow crab spider waits motionless for a pollinator to land. Shaped like a miniature marine crab, it assumes the color of the surface from which it hunts. Employing the adaptive use of camouflage provides the spider success as a predator and escape as prey.

Silent and rarely seen, we take minimal notice of spiders and their elaborate artwork. Today, standing among their intricate weavings exposed by a mist-filled morning, they seem to be everywhere. Strands of silk, laden with iridescent droplets, surround me with wonder.

Return to the Skies

In the fall of 1983, I traveled four hours to see a bald eagle. In those days, eagles were a rare sight in Massachusetts, and the last record of eagles nesting in the state was in 1905. Efforts were made to bring eagles back by transporting eaglets from Michigan's Upper Peninsula to the Quabbin Reservoir in central Massachusetts. Eagle chicks were raised on "hacking" platforms overlooking this 25,000-acre flooded valley and released into the wild. At that time, Quabbin Reservoir was the best place to go in the northeast to see this majestic bird. After a long drive, I had a great hike along the reservoir rim, but on that day, I didn't see any eagles.

Shortly after I returned to my home on Cape Cod, I heard about an eagle sighting at the landfill in Provincetown, not far from where I lived in Truro. Opportunistic predators and part-time scavengers, eagles show up for food, be it in a wilderness area or at a dump. During my visit to the landfill, I saw more than my share of gulls, yet once again, I didn't see any eagles. Four years passed before I saw my first bald eagle flying high over the trail to Sunfish Pond in New Jersey's Delaware Water Gap.

Flash forward forty years to a day in May. My wife and I were headed to Delaware to celebrate our anniversary by doing what we love best, exploring natural areas. We packed up our binoculars, spotting scope, bird and wildflower guides, and a picnic lunch, then set off all smiles chatting about possible sightings. Our destination was Bombay Hook National Wildlife Refuge which has an auto trail that moves between a variety of habitats, including wetlands, maritime forest, freshwater impoundments, and tidal flats. Two hours later, we began our slow crawl along the trail, gravel and shell fragments crunching beneath the tires. Windows down, breezes blowing, our frequent stops produced sightings of long-legged waders, sandpipers, waterfowl, gulls, and terns. We welcomed their raucous calls sounding at once like announcements and demands. Moving along a stretch of exposed tidal flats, we spotted twenty bald eagles. Some stood on the gravel bar, others flew in low to land beside them, and several tore at the flesh of fish recently caught. It was mesmerizing. There were four or five adults flanked by numerous first- and second-year birds. We had never seen so many bald eagles in one place before. When we finally tore ourselves away from that sight, we were treated to even more sightings of eagles as they soared in the sky and settled into the trees that dotted the marshes. We were thrilled. This day has long been remembered.

In 1963, spotters at Hawk Mountain Sanctuary observed a total of twenty bald eagles for the entire season. Sixty years later, the total increased to 619 birds. In 1963, there were only 417 known nesting pairs in the lower forty-eight states, while today there are more than 70,000 nesting pairs and more than 300,000 individual birds. After two episodes in the twentieth century that almost led to extinction, the eagles are making a remarkable comeback. Many scientists believe that the current population rivals its size in the early days of the colonies.

Bald eagles are endemic to North America. Their home range includes Canada, the United States, and Mexico. Most people think that the bald eagle is our national bird. However, neither congress nor any president to date has ever made it official. They declared the bison our national mammal, the oak our national tree, and the rose our national flower. Although the bald eagle was placed on the great seal of the United States in 1782, it has not received official status.

I've observed bald eagles migrating along the Appalachian Ridge while at Hawk Mountain Sanctuary in Pennsylvania. I've watched them soar over the sand dunes of the Cape May peninsula in New Jersey. Younger individuals will migrate first beginning in late August into September. Older adults that nested farther north move through during the months of November through December. Some bald eagles, especially those in the mid-Atlantic states, stick around for the winter and make up a year-round population.

The common name, bald eagle, finds its origin in the English word "balde," meaning white-headed. The Latin name, *Haliaeetus leucocephalus*, translates to white-headed sea eagle—sea (hali), eagle (aeetos), white (leukos), and head (cephalos). Known for the distinctive white coloration of the head and tail, bald eagle adults acquire these white feathers during their fourth or fifth year. The juveniles have varied shades of chocolate-brown feathers including those on their heads and tails. First year birds have a streaking of white feathers notable on their breasts and under the wings. This white coloration increases on second year birds. Male and female birds, identical in plumage, differ in size as females are generally twenty-five percent larger than males. Unlike golden eagles whose legs are covered in burnished brown feathers, bald eagles lack feathers on their lower legs and feet.

The beak color of a juvenile is black, changing in time to become the yellow color of the adult. Powerful and hooked, an eagle's beak can tear through fur, scales, feathers, and flesh into the body cavity of its prey. Strips of meat and bone are swallowed whole and move through the digestive system which both grinds food into smaller pieces and where much is absorbed by acids in the stomach. Any bone, fur, scales, or other undigestible material is formed into a pellet which the bird will spit out.

Bald eagles are built for soaring with a wingspan of six to seven and a half feet across. They rely on warm thermal air currents, rising from the earth's surface, to gain altitude. Their long, broad, slightly rounded wings are held at a right angle to the body as they move through the air. Rarely flapping, a single downbeat of their wings can propel them great distances.

Like many, I was surprised when I first heard the cry of a bald eagle. It was surprisingly high-pitched. Binoculars focused, I watched as the eagle thrust its head skyward to make a series of calls that declared its presence. Its cry made an indelible impression on me. Years later, remembering that sound, I was alerted to an eagle pair nesting only ten minutes from our home in suburban Philadelphia.

On a cold January morning, I was walking a path next to a swift-flowing creek. Hearing the now unmistakable call, I scanned the skies for a familiar silhouette. On this occasion, I could only hear its call and was not able to locate the bird. Still, I was sure it had to be an eagle. On my next walk along the trail and for months on-going, I was able to spot two of them on several occasions. Eventually, I saw them bringing food to the nest, which meant they were feeding young. On a mid-summer's day, I witnessed three large birds soaring above the wet meadow on the other side of the trail. At first glance, the three birds seemed to be flying together as a group, although their calls seemed to indicate distress. As they got closer, I realized there were two bald eagles chasing a turkey vulture. The eagles were closing in on the vulture when the one nearest dove to strike the vulture with its talons. Moments later the other eagle dove beneath the vulture, flipped over on its back and locked talons with the bird. Its flight interrupted, its abilities challenged, the vulture fled the area. The eagles continued to soar until the nuisance was a speck on the horizon.

Bald eagles build some of the largest stick nests of any birds, typically five to six feet wide and sometimes extending up to eight feet across. The nests are generally three to four feet high, though some are taller, and can weigh up to two tons. Adults will often return to the nest built the year prior. Together, the male and female will make repairs and add new materials to the nest. Mosses, grasses, lichens, and algae are arranged to form the lining in preparation for future young. Nesting begins in winter and generally ends in the latter months of summer when the fledglings leave the nest.

Throughout the centuries, the relationship between humans and bald eagles has been mixed. Indigenous American communities view eagles as messengers that carry the prayers of the people. It is felt that of all the creatures, eagles have the closest relationship to the Creator. In contrast, the white settlers viewed the eagle as a threat to their poultry and livestock. Although primarily fish eaters, eagles will occasionally eat birds and small mammals, including chickens, lambs, and calves. They rarely take an animal weighing more than thirty pounds. In the early twentieth century, a bounty was paid for a pair of eagle talons to keep the population under control.

During World War II, DDT was successfully used to kill a variety of insects that spread lethal diseases to the troops and the surrounding civilians. Especially troublesome in the Pacific Theater was the mosquito-borne illness of malaria. Thousands of troops were infected and many lost to the disease. Once DDT was implemented and found to be highly successful, a war on insects had begun in earnest. After WWII, Americans were assaulted with advertising campaigns promoting the notion that the best insect is a dead insect. DDT was liberally applied to crops, suburban yards, victory gardens, and even found permeating wallpaper for home use. This indiscriminate use of a "miracle" pesticide fomented a host of problems for humans and wildlife. Significant declines in bald eagle populations motivated scientists to action. Their studies revealed that high levels of DDT in eagles had led to the laying of paper-thin eggs. These fragile eggs would crack under the weight of the brooding adult birds, destroying the eggs and any chance for the next generation. Research showed that toxins from DDT had built up in the eagle's blood with each contaminated prey item eaten. Their food chain had been poisoned. While not toxic enough to kill the adult birds, it prohibited their ability to procreate. DDT was banned in 1972, ten years after the publication of *Silent Spring* by Rachel Carson. In addition, landmark environmental legislation passed in the early 1970s, including the Clean Air Act, the Clean Water Act, and the Endangered Species Act, contributed to saving the bald eagles.

Some individuals have taken extraordinary measures to help ensure a future for these birds. In 1979, a fifty-three-year-old Florida woman named Doris Mager, a vice-president for the Florida Audubon Society, spent six days and nights living in an abandoned bald eagle nest to call attention to the plight of the bird. Although she had never scaled a tree before, she hoisted herself to the fifty-foot summit. Food was sent up to her each day via a pulley system operated by volunteers and friends. In return, Doris would send down a coffee can which she used as a chamber pot. Through her efforts, Doris raised the needed funds to open the Audubon Center for Birds of Prey, a wildlife rehabilitation center in Maitland, Florida.

Given protection through legislation and the banning of DDT, bald eagle populations were able to recover. They were delisted as endangered in 2007. To this day, they are still protected under the Migratory Bird Treaty and the Bald and Golden Eagle Protection Act. Many scientists believe the eagles still need the additional protection that comes with being listed as endangered.

After several bouts on the edge of extinction, there is a glimmer of hope in the autumn air. Sitting on a rocky outcrop at Hawk Mountain on a mid-September morning, I witness eight bald eagles soaring along the mountain ridge over the course of three hours. Gliding with outstretched wings, they remind me that the policies and actions of humans can make a significant difference in protecting wildlife. In the nick of time, we have rescued an animal that was in serious trouble. We need to continue our vigilance to ensure its survival in the future. In the words of Rosalie Edge, founder of the Hawk Mountain Sanctuary, "The time to protect a species is while it is still common."

The Secret Migration

Across the narrows flowing between Maine's Hog Island Audubon Camp and the mainland, there is a small fresh-water pond teeming with life. It sits halfway up the gravel road in the middle of a grassy field scattered with wildflowers. During my twenty-five years working at the camp, "Pond Explorations" was always a top-tier activity.

The group met on the porch of the Queen Mary lab adjacent to the dock. A brief overview of pond habitat, including pictures of plants and animals, focused the group on what they might find. Equipment was then distributed to eager volunteers. Shouldering long-handled dip nets, strainers, large buckets, enamel pans, collecting cups, bug boxes, and field guides, we boarded the boat that would take us to the mainland. Typically, groups might find at least ten species of aquatic insects and a variety of frogs and salamanders. However, on one occasion, a camper netted a giant creature out of the pond muck that scared the daylights out of us. At first, it looked like a long gray snake until we noticed its ribbon-like fin, which began behind the head, wrapping around the tail and continuing underneath its body. When we touched the animal, it was slippery and slimy, unlike snakes which have dry leathery skin.

This was not a snake. It was a four-foot-long American eel, *Anguilla rostrata*. "Where did this come from?"

We often think of fish as either living in fresh or salt water. However, there are species of fish that move between fresh and saltwater. Anadromous fish, like salmon, herring, and shad, are born in freshwater ponds and rivers. They swim downstream to spend most of their lives in saltwater where they mature into adults. They return to their freshwater birthplaces when it is time to spawn and lay their eggs. Equally impressive are catadromous fish who reverse this process by hatching in saltwater, moving to fresh, and returning as adults to spawn in saltwater. This is the case with the American eels who begin their lives in saltwater, then make their way to bays and estuaries. Some stay in the estuaries and others move upriver where they may spend ten to thirty years as yellow eels before becoming sexually mature silver eels. When it's time to spawn and lay eggs, American eels return to their saltwater birthplace, the Sargasso Sea within the Atlantic Ocean.

The life history of the American eel eluded many until the early part of the twentieth century. In the fourth century B.C.E., Aristotle believed that eels arose spontaneously "out of the earth's guts" from the mud and moist ground. After many dissections, he was unable to find eggs or reproductive organs, so he felt this was the only plausible explanation.

By the first century C.E., Pliny the Elder, who authored thirty-seven volumes of Natural History detailing his careful observations, wrote that eels produced offspring by rubbing their skins against rocks and other submerged objects. During the Middle Ages, eels were believed to have evolved from long pieces of horsehair. Thus, the discovery of the American eel's spawning ground in the early part of the twentieth century and its arduous migration journey endures as an extraordinary example of dedicated scientific detective work.

For years, scientists had been familiar with a tiny, translucent leaf-shaped fish named *Leptocephalus* (lepto for leaf, cephalis for head). In 1895, two Italian biologists placed this fish in a saltwater aquarium to observe its feeding habits. After eating for several days, *Leptocephalus* suddenly stopped eating and began to shrink. As its size diminished, its body changed dramatically from the shape of a willow leaf to an elongated, wormlike body. The creature was easily identified as an elver, or young freshwater eel.

At the turn of the last century, a young Danish biologist named Johannes Schmidt spent eighteen years sailing around the world, determined to track down the spawning ground of the eel. Schmidt captured *Leptocephalus* larvae of varying sizes from many different parts of the world. While sailing in the Sargasso Sea, he discovered *Leptocephalus* larvae that were only a quarter inch long, the smallest ever discovered. He reasoned that these must be newly hatched fish.

The Sargasso Sea is a place of legend situated in the northwestern Atlantic Ocean, east of Florida and on the western fringes of Bermuda. The only sea without any land borders, the Sargasso Sea is surrounded by four major ocean currents that move clockwise around it. Within these currents lies a gyre of unusually calm, warm, deep blue water approximately the size of the continental United States. There is little wind, few clouds, and the water seems motionless. Long feared by sailors, the Sargasso Sea is often referred to as "the island of lost ships," possibly based on its location within the doldrums of the Horse Latitudes combined with the rafts of dense seaweeds. The world's largest concentration of brown algae known as *Sargassum*, named after the Sargasso itself, flourishes in great mats, sometimes miles long. The *Sargassum* branches are dotted with gas-filled berry-like structures containing oxygen. These air sacs allow the plant to float freely on the surface of the water, colliding with other plants to form dense tangles. A wide variety of marine creatures use this seaweed as a home, nursery, or spawning ground. Here, beneath this huge mat of algae, lies what is believed to be the birthplace of both the American and European eel.

Scientists believe that eels spawn during the months of December through May, although this has never been observed. We know that the larvae, once hatched, rise to the ocean surface, joining the larger free floating plankton community. During this first year of life, many of the young eels are lost to predation by fish and other marine animals. Those that survive enter the Gulf Stream which carries them across the Atlantic to North America's coastal waters. By the time they reach the Mid-Atlantic and New England coasts, the leaf-shaped larvae are approximately three inches long. Their transparent bodies have transformed into the familiar snake-like shape of an eel complete with fins and tail. Referred to as glass eels, they continue their migration, seeking the freshwater of rivers, ponds, and lakes.

Once the glass eels reach four inches in length, they turn yellowish in color and are referred to as elvers. They travel by the thousands up tidal waterways and, when necessary, for brief periods of time, over land. Their ability to leave the water and navigate across land is enabled by the mucous membrane covering their skin. This membrane keeps them moist and allows them to absorb oxygen.

Young elvers are frequently seen traveling upstream in the spring, and adult eels are easily observed heading downstream in the fall. In fact, the migration of eels occurs in practically every harbor, estuary, and tidal marsh along the east coast. However, to this day, mating behavior has never been observed, despite diligent efforts by teams of scientists exploring the Sargasso Sea.

Eels are nocturnal animals, hunting and traveling at night. Daylight hours are spent buried in the mud, underneath rocks, or hidden among organic debris. It is possible to find them in unlikely places, such as wells and ponds with no visible inlet. They are found in the Great Lakes, reached by way of the Saint Lawrence Seaway, and traveling the tributaries of the Mississippi River watershed to places as far away as Minnesota.

After spending ten to thirty years in freshwater, the eel reaches its adult size and changes color from a yellowish ocher to a bronzed dark gray. Upon reaching sexual maturity, an eel reverses course to return to its saltwater birthplace. Internal physical changes take place, including the disintegration of its digestive tract and the enlargement of blood vessels surrounding the swim bladder. Research has not determined when eels become male or female, although factors including temperature or population density may play a role. Adult males are smaller than females, which can be up to forty-eight inches in length. Once they have reached the Sargasso Sea, a single female can lay between ten and twenty million eggs, which are fertilized externally by a male.

Once spawning has taken place, the adults die, and the eggs float to the surface, where they hatch to repeat the life cycle of their parents.

We have uncovered more about the lifecycle of the eel than Pliny could ever imagine, though there remain many unanswered questions. Once the eels leave our shores, they drop out of sight completely. No one has successfully followed an eel as it moves between destinations. Tiny location devices applied to their bodies have garnered little success. Signals were soon lost and little data gained. Their comings and goings in a nutrient-rich saltwater world remain a mystery. Left with a host of unanswered questions, research persists. What triggers their return to saltwater? How do they navigate thousands of miles of open water to return to the Sargasso Sea? Do they have an internal compass, use underwater geological landmarks, or sense chemical properties of the water? Can they taste or smell familiar currents?

The campers circled around the "find" of the day—eyes wide, wonder palpable. The eel was placed in a large bucket of pondwater with a net tightly draped over the top. We watched it move side to side, generating waves that traveled the length of its body. For approximately three minutes, time stopped for the fifteen pairs of eyes mesmerized by a creature they had never seen before. When we removed the net, the eel slithered out of the bucket onto the grass and slipped back into the pond. Soon, it would head out on a journey, thousands of miles long, to the Sargasso Sea.

Autumnal Pool Party

I'll never forget my first encounter with a vernal pool at my college nature preserve in Ohio. We were hiking through the forest on a mild day in mid-March. There was still snow on the ground, though it was quickly melting and cascading down the hillsides. We came upon a low area filled with water and stopped to take a closer look. I had read about the value of these small ephemeral bodies of water to wildlife, yet I had never stopped to examine one. I was spellbound. The water was alive with countless tiny creatures, some no bigger than a pinhead and nothing larger than an inch across. Tiny water fleas (*Daphnia*) hopped through the water with jerky, abrupt movements. Water boatmen darted in the water column, propelled by their oar-like hindlegs. Translucent fairy shrimp swam upside down, using their eleven pair of appendages for swimming, breathing, and feeding. And most surprising of all, there was a tiny dark salamander with feathery gills behind its head. White specks dotted its sides.

The internet hadn't been invented yet, so I couldn't use a web browser to identify the salamander. When I got back to my room, I searched through my books to find one that could help me identify it. It wasn't long before I found a field guide to reptiles and amphibians. Pouring through the pages, I realized that it only showed pictures of animals as adults, and I did not see any salamanders resembling the one I discovered earlier.

It would take thirty years before I realized that I had possibly found the larval stage of a marbled salamander.

Like the spotted and tiger salamanders, the marbled salamander is part of the mole salamander family, a group of subterranean creatures that spend the day under logs, stones, and boards or in underground passageways. These places offer moist environments and protection from harm. Venturing out under the cover of darkness, they search for earthworms, insects, and other macroinvertebrates. To ward off predators, they secrete a mild toxin through their skin that gives them a foul taste and makes them slippery and slimy.

The best time to see most species of mole salamanders is on a dark, wet night in early spring. This is when they emerge from their winter torpor, work their way to the surface, and head to aquatic habitats to breed. Not so for the marbled salamanders. They breed and lay their eggs months earlier, in the fall, on dry land. The females seek depressions in the earthen floor that will eventually fill with rainwater. Their eggs must be submerged so that their larvae can begin their lives in water.

During the months of September and October, the male heads down to a dry wetland area that will fill with water during fall and spring rains. When the female arrives, they shuffle and posture beneath the leaf litter. Eventually, she picks up a sperm packet deposited by the male and draws it into her body. Once fertilization has occurred, the female seeks a nest site somewhere between the deepest and shallowest area of the depression. This prevents premature hatching of her eggs during a minor rain and ensures that enough water will be available for the larvae. She will lay between thirty and two hundred eggs beneath the moist vegetation and debris. While most amphibians lay their eggs in jelly-like masses, the marbled salamanders lay individual eggs, tiny transparent jewels resembling miniature crystal balls. Over time, with exposure to the elements, these tiny eggs, less than three millimeters wide, blend with the soil and leaf litter at the bottom of their autumnal pool. Unlike most amphibians, the mother stays with her eggs, curling her body around them. In this way, she protects her eggs from predators and keeps them moist until the depression fills with water. During most years, a major rain event in September or October fills the depression with rainwater, submerging the eggs and enabling them to hatch in a few days. Throughout the winter months, the larvae remain surprisingly active, feeding and growing underneath the ice on zooplankton and macroinvertebrates. On warmer days, when the ice melts, they are free to swim in the open water. Should the rains of autumn fail to fill the pool, the eggs overwinter and hatch months later when the pool fills with the rains of spring. In this case, the mother stays with her eggs in autumn until cold temperatures force her to move on to a winter burrow below the frostline. Although eggs brooded by the mother have a higher survival rate, abandoned eggs can still be successful.

There are many hypotheses about why the marbled salamander's life cycle differs from that of other mole salamanders. Hatching in fall ensures that marbled salamander larvae have a head start. They can feed with little competition, which in turn has allowed them to grow older and stronger than their counterparts. Fewer predators prowl their pools at this time of year, granting an additional layer of safety and longevity. Once the warm wet days of spring arrive, the young marbled will prey on the larvae of spotted salamanders, spring peepers, chorus frogs, and wood frogs, along with feeding on aquatic worms, small invertebrates, and zooplankton. Little is known about the activity of adult marbled salamanders after waking in spring; however, we do know that they aren't seeking breeding pools.

The life cycle of the marbled salamander is completely intertwined with the fluctuations of water in these temporary seasonal pools. Additional snow melt and early spring rainfall provide the perfect environment for the larvae's continued growth. Pools that dry up in the summer cannot support fish and other predators that might eat the larvae. Upon reaching the juvenile stage, they leave their pools to spend the summer hidden in the surrounding forest. It can take up to fifteen months for the juveniles to fully mature.

Over the years, I've had several encounters with marbled salamander larvae in early spring. However, the sighting of an adult had remained elusive. They range from northern Florida to southern New Hampshire and west to southern Illinois and eastern parts of Texas and Oklahoma, but they are rarely seen. I finally found one a few years ago on a trip to the Great Smoky Mountains in Tennessee. Hidden beneath a rotting log in the Cades Cove region of the park, I found the salamander I was most anxious to see. As it was chunky and compact with a stubby tail and bold white bands across its dark body, I knew that this animal was unmistakably a male marbled salamander. The females are larger and have grayish bands on their bodies. After moistening my hands, I carefully picked him up to get a better look. Lifting his small body close to my face, I was mesmerized. Gazing eye to eye, I reflected on how fortunate I was to be in the presence of such a remarkable creature.

Human understanding of the natural world is often based on broad generalizations and the creation of distinct categories. Marbled salamanders remind us that other animals operate by their own rules and don't always fit into our constructs. I am reminded of the words of Henry Beston, author of *The Outermost House*: "In a world older and more complete than ours, they move finished and complete, gifted with extensions of the senses we have lost or never obtained, living by voices we shall never hear."

Nighttime Aerialists

Several years ago, one of my students found an injured bat and brought it to school. He was hoping I would be able to help. Nestled in a shoe box, lying in the folds of a soft towel, was a small brown bat with a drooping wing. As it lay on its side, two tiny black eyes met mine. "What's wrong with you?" I thought. "What happened?" Others gathered around us to see the bat and to hear what I thought. It was obvious to me that we were going to need someone familiar with bats to help this little guy. I called a local wildlife rehabilitation center to see if they could help. They told me that, by law, they were not allowed to handle a bat in Pennsylvania and referred me to a center in New Jersey. Pennsylvania's policy has its roots in the belief that most bats carry rabies. To the contrary, studies indicate that less than one percent of our bat population are carriers, while ninety-four percent of rabies cases involve cattle, dogs, and cats. After contacting the New Jersey center, I arranged for someone to cover my classes and drove across state lines to begin the rehabilitation of the little brown bat. When I returned to school later that day, my students were relieved to hear that the bat would be assessed and we would receive a report within the next forty-eight hours. Two days later, upon speaking with the rehabilitator, I was able to share the news that they had examined the bat and determined it had a broken wing bone. A tiny splint was created and applied to stabilize the fragile finger-like bone. Over the next ten to fourteen days, the bat would be kept quiet, immobilized, and fed, after which the odds were good that it could be successfully released. The students were overjoyed to hear the good news.

Although bats may look a lot like mice, they are not rodents and most likely evolved from tree-dwelling animals resembling shrews and moles. Though these mammals were present toward the end of the dinosaur era, there are no fossils of the evolved bats following the extinction of the dinosaurs. Still, between fifty-two and fifty-five million years ago, during the Eocene period, fossil evidence indicates that there was a sudden explosion of bats, with many species discovered worldwide.

Every October, several weeks before bat cut-outs appear in elementary school windows, three species of wild bats in the northeast begin their southern migration. The silver-haired bat, eastern red bat, and hoary bat, all solitary in nature, prepare to leave their roosts beneath the foliage of trees and bark. They travel hundreds of miles in search of warmer climes where insects are once again abundant. Meanwhile, species of social bats, including the little brown bat, the tricolored bat, and the big brown bat, move from their summer haunts in the forest to form colonies in local caves, mine shafts, and old buildings where they will hibernate throughout the winter months.

When the days grow ever shorter in late summer and early fall, bats are easily spotted flying at twilight. As the only flying mammal, they use their supple wings for a variety of tasks, including the pursuit of prey. Flying squirrels can glide for short distances using ample folds of skin attached between their fore and back legs. However, when it comes to flying mammals, bats are in a class of their own. Close inspection of a bat's wing reveals five long, thin finger bones, placing them in the order Chiroptera, Greek for "hand-wing." These bones are covered with a membrane that stretches between each long finger bone and its many movable joints. Powerful muscles in the bat's back and chest move its wings down, reducing air resistance, and up, producing lift. Unlike birds whose bones are hollow, the bones of bats are solid. Were they to stand for periods of time, the weight of their bodies would result in bone-crushing physical compression. Instead, they use their clawed feet to hang upside down when resting and when giving birth. Additionally, the upside-down position makes it easier to take flight.

Worldwide, there are more than 1400 known species of bats, making up a quarter of the world's mammals. Forty-five species are found in the United States and Canada. By contrast, there are 112 bat species in Costa Rica, a country the size of West Virginia. Bats range in size from the bumblebee bat, a little over an inch in length, to the flying fox, with a wingspan up to six feet. All the bats in the northeast are insectivorous. A single bat can eat a thousand insects in one hour. In other parts of the world, there are bats that feed on fish, nectar, fruit, and blood. Over 500 plant species rely on bats for pollination and the spreading of plant seeds, including mango, banana, peach, guava, agave (for making tequila), and cacao (for making chocolate).

Despite their reputation for being blind, bats have sensitive vision and can see quite well under "pitch black" conditions. Their sharp focus during the fading light of dusk is due to the high density of rods located in their retinas. Like the function of rods in our eyes, they gather low amounts of light, enabling a bat to receive information about the environment around it. Insectivorous bats use echolocation as their principal mode of navigation to both find food and avoid obstacles. They emit sound waves that bounce off an object and back to their sensitive ears. The frequency and repetition of their calls depends on intent. Lower frequencies cover long distances, while higher pitched calls deliver more detail. Bats also issue calls promoting social interactions, avoiding obstacles, and locating prey.

Despite unfounded superstitions, bats are known for their cleanliness and hygiene. Typically, a bat spends more than an hour each day washing itself. If it can't reach part of its body with its tongue, it uses the saliva-moistened thumbs on its wings or the wings themselves. It will frequently scratch the back of its head with its feet, licking the feet afterwards.

As flying nocturnal mammals, bats have stirred imaginations throughout history. We have created legends, myths, and stories to define an animal so physically and behaviorally unique. Indigenous American tribes held various spiritual beliefs about bats. The Navajo spoke of bats as messengers between different worlds, bridging the natural and supernatural. The Apache, Creek, and Cherokee told stories about flightless mice that convinced the birds to give them wings. European settlers brought their many fearful ideas about bats with them to America.

Having observed bats flying out of caves, they associated them with the underworld and the foretelling of death. Bram Stoker's *Dracula*, published in 1897, introduced us to the transformation of fictitious vampires into blood-thirsty wolves and bats. The twentieth-century hero Batman cast bats in a more positive light, albeit having nothing to do with the mammal itself. The weeks leading up to Halloween offers teachers and concerned citizens a terrific opportunity to share information about bats. Bat Conservation International, an organization dedicated to stop the extinction of bat populations, provides a website full of scientific and conservation efforts we can share—facts instead of fables.

Living in an old farmhouse, we shared our home with little brown bats. We occasionally saw them flying erratically at dusk, chasing insects. They never seemed bothered by our presence, and we were happy to see them around. There were occasions when we would find one during the day resting in the eaves above our porch. Its chosen location was usually only feet from our door. Since bats are wild animals, we knew to keep a respectable distance. Needing to use the entrance and pass by the bat in doing so, my wife and I discussed our approach to the door. Our two-year-old daughter became restless and questioned our hesitation. To quell any possible fears, we named the bat after one of our most affable friends. We called the bat Bert. Our daughter loved our friend Bert and consequently greeted the bat each time we passed. There was a time or two when our approach was not as thoughtful as it should have been, and we were reprimanded by a scolding hiss.

Sadly, thirteen species of hibernating bats lost as much as ninety percent of their population when a fungal disease, known as white-nosed syndrome, first showed up in a cave in upstate New York in 2006. It is believed that the disease was initially spread by visitors to caves who unwittingly transported it on their infected gear and clothing. Appearing as a white fuzzy coating on their muzzles, ears, and wings, the fungus wakes infected bats during hibernation. This interruption triggers the depletion of limited fat reserves and can result in dehydration, starvation, and death. White-nosed syndrome is epidemic in scale, infecting large colonies and proving to be one of the worst wildlife disease outbreaks in North American history. The little brown bat, once the most common bat in North America, is now an endangered species. The closure of populated caves and mine shafts to human visitors has provided more protection for the bats and resulted in a modest increase in their populations.

Today, there are many who are working to counter the negative myths and superstitions surrounding bats. In many school classrooms and through public program offerings, children are introduced to the vital role bats play as members of forest and cave communities. When my daughter was in kindergarten, one of her favorite stuffed animals was a bat named Stellaluna, the fictional fruit bat from the award-winning children's book by the same name. The author, Janell Cannon, while working in a library, noted that there weren't many children's books about bats. In fact, there were only three, and two were in bad shape. She felt the need to write something that would dispel the negativity associated with bats and cast them in their true light. Several years and many drafts later, Janell finalized the illustrations and text of her picture book. Young learners were now able to view bats through a lens of empathy.

There are things that each of us can do to support bats in our areas. Planting gardens with native perennials that entice pollinating insects and eliminating our use of pesticides is a great way to start. We can provide shelters for them in the form of bat boxes where they can roost, mate, and have their young. A quick survey of lighting around our homes can produce opportunities to dim some of the light during the summer and fall months. Given the infectious nature of white-nosed fungus, it is important to stay out of caves where bats could be hibernating.

During twilight walks, I frequently see bats flying through my neighborhood. They are not as common as they were twenty years ago, still there are days when I speculate that the numbers might be increasing. Hopefully, our efforts to learn about and protect these irreplaceable creatures will bring them back in greater numbers. Bats provide important ecological services, including pollination, seed dispersal, and insect control, and they are a vital part of terrestrial and aquatic ecosystems. We need to return the favor and protect these glorious nighttime aerialists.

King and Queen of the Butterflies

I spent the day sitting on a rocky outcrop at Hawk Mountain's North Lookout. Binoculars in hand, I joined hundreds of enthusiastic people of all ages eager to observe the autumnal hawk migration. Two species of raptors dominated the day, the sharp-shinned hawk and the Cooper's hawk, both known for their extraordinary speed and agility when hunting small birds. Their short, broad wings and narrow tails make them ideally suited for pursuing prey in the forest. When out in the open, they do not soar over vast distances like the larger hawks, but rather alternate between a series of flaps and glides. If I didn't see anything else besides these magnificent birds of prey, I would have been satisfied. But there were more ... bald eagles, osprey, red-tailed hawks, red-shouldered hawks, and kestrels. Yet, the highlight of my day wasn't even a bird. It was an insect. Delicate orange and black wings floated alongside the steep rocky lookout. I was witnessing the migration of monarch butterflies journeying south, following the same mountain ridges and using the same air currents as the hawks. They were heading miles away to forests they had never known.

A monarch butterfly, weighing less than a gram, can fly as far as three thousand miles. Butterflies are literally powered by the sun. Unlike birds, the majority of which migrate at night, a butterfly only flies during the day when the sun is shining. Butterflies are ectotherms (cold-blooded) and are unable to flap their wings when the temperature falls below fifty-five degrees. During cool autumn evenings, they roost in large congregations, preferably in pine, cedar, and fir trees. There are several species of butterflies that fly south for the winter, including painted ladies, red admirals, and buckeyes. The monarch, however, is the only species known to complete a two-way migration. Those born east of the Rockies funnel into a small mountainous area in central Mexico. Those born in the west coast states cluster at sites along California's Monterey peninsula. Meanwhile, there are populations in Florida, the Caribbean, Central America, South America, Australia, India, western Europe, and some Pacific islands that are nonmigratory.

It took thirty-nine years of detective work, aided by thousands of volunteers, to locate the destination of the northeast's migrating monarch butterflies. Dr. Fred Urquhart and his wife Norah, at the University of Toronto, created tiny gummed labels that were applied to the wings of monarchs. Deemed the alar tagging method, the *ala* being Latin for wing, each tag was printed with the message, "Send to Zoology University Toronto Canada." Boxes of found tagged monarchs began arriving from parts of Canada and the United States. Energized by the success of this project, Norah wrote an article in 1952 about their research and solicited the help of volunteers. Her request eventually motivated thousands of volunteers who joined in the effort to track the southbound route of the monarchs. Initial findings tracked the butterflies no further than the state of Texas. Later, after trips to the eastern and western United States and south to the Gulf of Mexico, Norah again took to publishing articles. This time, her articles targeted Mexican newspapers, looking for volunteers to tag and to report sightings. In 1975, the Urquharts received the phone call they had been hoping for. American engineer and amateur naturalist Kenneth Brugger and his wife, Catalina, had made a thrilling discovery while working in Mexico. High in the Sierra Madres along the Transvolcanic Belt of central Mexico, they found millions of monarch butterflies clinging to the branches and trunks of oyamel fir trees. The sight of millions upon millions of butterflies was breathtaking. Eager to walk among the monarchs themselves, the Urquharts traveled to Mexico the following year. As they stood surrounded by fluttering wings and trees pendulous with orange and black butterflies, a branch heavy laden with monarchs broke and fell to the ground. Dr. Urquhart moved to pick up the branch so that the butterflies underneath might survive. As he did so, he noticed a monarch with a white tag on its wing. This individual had been tagged by a volunteer in Minnesota and flew all the way to this Mexican forest.

Why do monarchs travel such long distances? Insect-eating birds fly south where food is plentiful. However, monarchs eat little to no food while wintering in Mexico. Whales migrate south so their calves can begin their lives in warmer waters. If the butterflies were looking for warmth, they wouldn't head to the mountains at an elevation nearly two miles above sea level. It seems that their flight to this region in Mexico, which is only seventy-three miles wide, provides the perfect microclimate.

Within the oyamel fir forests of the Transvolcanic Belt, there are approximately ten to twelve clusters of monarchs. Categorized as cloud forests, they are regularly immersed in fog and low-lying clouds, ensuring adequate humidity and water to drink. The temperature is warm enough to keep the butterflies from freezing yet cool enough to allow them to burn their fat reserves slowly. The protective branches of the oyamel trees provide roosts, and the nearby trees and shrubs shield them from harsh winter weather. Arriving in November, the monarchs attach to the oyamel's branches in tightly packed layers to keep warm. A single tree can hold thousands of semidormant butterflies.

The warming temperatures and increasing daylight hours of March stimulate activity and restore the butterfly's reproductive drive. They leave their roosts in search of nectar to fuel their journey north. Breeding can again take place to produce the second generation. The females search for milkweed, and once the plants have been found, they begin laying their eggs. When the offspring reach the adult stage, they continue the long journey northward, repeating the cycle as they go. It will take the birth of two more generations before the monarchs arrive in the northern United States and Canada.

The monarch butterfly moves through four stages of development, also known as complete metamorphosis: egg, larva, pupa, and adult. Their eggs are creamy white in color, about the size of a pin head, and bear symmetrical vertical striations which can only be seen under magnification. The female lays one egg at a time on the underside of milkweed leaves. A few days later, the eggs turn gray as the tiny caterpillar forms inside, and in four to six days, the eggs are ready to hatch.

The caterpillar is so small it can hardly be seen, but it grows quickly on an exclusive diet of milkweed leaves. Initially, it appears pale green to grayish white and somewhat translucent. As it increases in size, the larva takes on the characteristic white, black, and yellow stripes. During this two-week period, from hatching to forming a chrysalis, the larva moves through a series of five instars, shedding its outgrown skin as it grows ever larger. By the time it is ready to form a chrysalis, it can measure two inches or more in length.

Just before the last instar, the caterpillar stops feeding and searches for a safe place to form its chrysalis. It may choose to use the same milkweed plant or to wander off to find a suitable plant nearby. Here, on the underside of a leaf or twig, the caterpillar weaves a spare silken mat and attaches itself with the tiny hook on its tail, called the cremaster. Hanging upside down in the shape of the letter *J*, it is ready to shed its skin one last time to begin the pupal stage. As the skin splits apart, beginning at the head, a soft and smooth lime green form is revealed. It hardens to become a delicate jade jewel rimmed at the top with a horizontal golden line. This is the chrysalis, where the monarch spends nine to fourteen days changing into a butterfly. Approximately twenty-four hours prior to hatching, the chrysalis becomes transparent, and you can glimpse the orange and black wings of the butterfly inside. Upon emergence, referred to as eclose, it rests upside down, unfolding its body and pumping fluid from its enlarged abdomen into its wings. After drying for several hours, it is ready to set off in search of wildflower nectar.

Thirty years ago, monarchs were abundant in milkweed fields across the northeast. Every September, I would collect a few caterpillars in the local fields around my house so my second graders could raise them in their classrooms. Recently, it has been so difficult to find them that I ordered caterpillars from Monarch Watch, a community science organization based at the University of Kansas. It is interesting to note that the Urquhart's Insect Migration Association was the citizen science predecessor of Monarch Watch.

Monarch caterpillars depend on milkweed as their sole food source. Adults sip the sweet nectar of milkweed flowers in addition to nectaring upon other plant species. Still, the females must lay their eggs exclusively on milkweed leaves. Out of seventy-three species of milkweed in the United States, there are thirty native species that monarchs regularly visit. Common milkweed, *Asclepias syriaca*, is the most prevalent species, followed by butterfly weed, *Asclepias tuberosa*, and swamp milkweed, *Asclepias incarnata*. Named for the sticky white sap that can be seen oozing from damaged leaves, milkweed contains cardiac glycosides. These compounds can affect heart function, making the butterfly toxic to most species of birds and mammals. The monarch's brilliant orange coloration serves as a warning to potential predators. Its coloration is so effective that the viceroy butterfly, bearing similar colors and patterns, is a known mimic of the monarch.

Milkweed seeds are encased in pods which split open as they dry. Nestled tightly inside the pod are numerous seeds, each attached to a tuft of fluff. Once caught by the wind, the tuft propels its seed into the air. Given good earth in an open field with plenty of sunlight and sufficient rainfall, a milkweed seed will sprout and grow.

In years past, milkweed was abundant in cornfields throughout the northeast. With the advent in the 1990s of genetically engineered corn that can tolerate the chemical glyphosate found in herbicides, farmers have increased their yields. However, milkweed can no longer grow in these treated corn fields, eliminating both the food and habitat necessary to sustain future generations.

In the past fifty years, meadows and grasslands have become the most endangered habitats in North America. Along with numerous bird species, including bobolinks and meadowlarks, monarchs depend on these open spaces for survival. Many fields have become sights for development and those that are left alone revert to forests.

Climate change can impact the butterfly's journey, both in its summer breeding sites and its wintering grounds. Hotter and drier summers in the north and colder winters in the south have contributed to population decline.

For many years, community scientists, like my second graders, have monitored the monarch population by participating in a tagging program. A tiny adhesive tag is placed on the mitten-shaped discal cell on the underside of the butterfly. Since it is close to the center of gravity for the butterfly, it does not impact its flight. Each tag has a number and the website of Monarch Watch. On our data sheet, we have the number for each butterfly, whether it is captive reared or wild, and whether it is male or female. Only the male has a black gland on the top surface of each hindwing, which produces a pheromone, or scent, for attracting the female. When butterflies with tags are recovered, scientists gain valuable information about their geographic distribution and the timing of migration.

At the south end of Hog Island, home to the Audubon Camp in Maine, there is a field adorned with milkweed. For many years, I've visited this spot with campers and enjoyed experiencing it through their eyes. We examine the plants with hand lenses and often find the creamy white eggs, the striking yellow, black, and white caterpillars, and the jewel-like chrysalides. Meanwhile, all around us, the orange and black butterflies flutter through the sun-drenched meadow.

Before it is too late, we need to do our part to protect this magnificent creature. We can start by preserving our milkweed fields, planting new milkweed, and filling our gardens with native perennials that produce the nectar upon which the adults depend. The king and queen of the butterflies need our help.

A Moment with a Falcon

Some of the most important lessons I've learned weren't taught in a classroom. As a teacher, I've devoted my career to offering the most engaging lessons possible. Though well intentioned and effective as I was, I learned years ago that there is no substitute for the deep impact of an unexpected mentor at a serendipitous moment.

It was a cold, damp, and windy Saturday afternoon, certainly not the sort of day when most people choose to be out for a walk. I was working at the Cape Cod Museum of Natural History, and it was part of my job to lead field walks for the public. Five hardy souls showed up for my fall wildflower walk. An hour before, I walked the area, field guide in hand, to make sure I could identify all the flowering plants. I wanted to give my participants accurate information—the goal of all teachers. As it turns out, I would not be the sole teacher, nor would the primary takeaway be about autumn blooms.

I began the walk by explaining why leaves change colors and identifying some of the goldenrod species in the area. As we crossed Stony Brook Marsh en route to the beech forest, a group of tree swallows flew by. One of the children on the walk interrupted me to find out what kind of birds they were. If I hadn't looked up at that very moment, I would have missed the whole thing. The episode lasted for no more than two seconds. Luckily, all six of us were facing the same direction, as there wasn't even time to tell someone to turn around and look.

The incident centered around a merlin, a fierce falcon mid-way in size between a mourning dove and a pigeon. Merlins are regularly seen on the Cape during the fall and spring migrations. During the summer, they

breed in the northern states and Canada. They winter in the southern states, Mexico, Central America, and South America. The male's back is blue-gray, while the larger female's back is brownish gray to dark brown. Like all falcons, the merlin has long pointed wings, an elongated narrow tail, a large head with a sharp hooked bill, and strong curved talons. With its streamlined body, it is a graceful, agile, and extremely fast flier. Medieval noblewomen Catherine the Great and Mary Queen of Scots hunted skylarks with merlins, and to this day, merlins are commonly used by falconers.

I knew that merlins fed primarily on small birds, especially sparrows caught on the wing. They can also take down larger birds, including pigeons, small ducks, and larger sandpipers along the coast. They've been seen diving for unsuspecting prey at speeds topping one hundred miles per hour. Amazingly, I've read that they can catch swallows and swifts, birds known for their speed on the wing. Yet, seeing is believing, and there it was, happening right before our eyes.

Out of nowhere, a merlin appeared overhead and caught one of the swallows in mid-flight. Clutching the swallow in its talons, it flew into the woods. My *Peterson Field Guide to Birds* describes the tree swallow's song as a "liquid twitter." Certainly, Mr. Peterson wasn't referring to the sound we heard coming from the talons of the falcon. Upon impact, there was a loud horror-stricken shriek followed by complete silence. It was the most breathtakingly frightful sound imaginable. I found it hard to believe that a bird so small could make such a loud sound. It didn't last long. The swallow's otherworldly vocalization lasted only a split second before the duo disappeared among the trees.

There are few animals that prey on swallows. Falcons possess the essential speed, strength, and agility. I assume that merlins catch swallows and other small birds on the wing all the time, even though I've only witnessed this once in my life. I've seen sharp-shinned hawks and Cooper's hawks grabbing small birds at feeding stations; however, these were stationary targets. To date, I have related this experience to many people, some of them avid birders, and haven't found anyone else who has witnessed a merlin catch a bird in flight. Truly, it was an exceptional few seconds. The participants on my walk and I were in the right place at the right time, experiencing what educators refer to as "the teachable moment."

In a television interview, the poet Robert Frost was asked if he thought nature was essentially kind. To the surprise of many people who revered him as a "nature poet," Frost responded that "nature is always more or less cruel." Perhaps Frost overstated things by calling nature cruel. Nature is simply indifferent to our judgments. Animals need to eat. Plants need sunlight, water, and air. Springs bubble up from the ground. Mountains erode over time. Life is always in process. We talk of systems, cycles, patterns, and connections to better understand the natural world, yet there is always the unexpected and unexplained.

Many years have passed, though I often think about that moment. As an outdoor educator, I am careful to scout out my walks, interspersing activities and interpretation. However, I always welcome the opportunity of changing course when the unexpected presents itself. I learned a lot from the merlin at Stony Brook Marsh.

Life After Labor Day

As in an expressive piece of music, there are crescendos and diminuendos in the wildflower world. Late March and early April feature a proliferation of spring ephemerals emerging beneath the bare branches of sun-drenched forests. Months later, in the days surrounding the summer solstice, the diversity of flowering plants peaks, or crescendos, in meadows and wetlands. In the intense heat of the mid-summer months, growth is tempered. There is a diminuendo of sorts as the world of wildflowers appears settled and steady. Mindful of these dynamics, our local botany club meets every month between April and October, with one exception, the August slowdown. Once Labor Day has passed, wildflower numbers and variety once again increase, reaching a crescendo around the fall equinox. Yellow, orange, red, blue, and purple flowers dot our fields and hedgerows like confetti.

The stars of our autumn floral display are the asters and goldenrods, members of the Asteraceae family, formerly the Compositae family. In fact, the family name comes from the Greek word for star. Each flower head consists of multiple individual disc and ray florets, sometimes hundreds, enclosed by a whorl of protective bracts. They are ideal nectar plants because they allow butterflies and other insects to conserve energy by sampling many flowers in a small area.

Resembling daisies, which predominantly grow in the spring, the fall-blooming asters have a smaller central disc and more color variations than daisies, which are generally white. Two of my favorite asters are the New York aster, *Symphyotrichum novi-belgii*, and the New England aster, *Symphyotrichum novae- angliae*. Both plants have perfect flowers, meaning they are composed of both male and female parts, and a yellow or reddish central disc surrounded by rays in shades of purple and pink.

The smaller New York aster has smooth narrow leaves that clasp its thin stem. The New England aster is taller with hairy lance-shaped leaves clasping a thicker stem. The flowers give way to achenes, the small, one-seeded fruits dispersed by the wind. Asters spread vegetatively along horizontal underground rootstalks called rhizomes.

Asters provide late-season nectar for a wide variety of pollinators, including honeybees, miner bees, syrphid flies, and monarch butterflies. The leaves are eaten by the pearl crescent and checkerspot butterfly larvae. As the winter season approaches, the partially grown caterpillars curl up inside the leaves, remaining in diapause, a stage of suspended development, through the winter.

Goldenrods provide late-season pollen and nectar for a wide variety of insect pollinators, including butterflies, bees, wasps, and beetles. Although often blamed for seasonal allergies, its colorful pollen, attractive to insects, is too heavy and sticky to be airborne. The real culprit is ragweed, whose pollen is light, dry, and easily carried on the wind. Ragweed flowers are tiny and inconspicuous, as there is no need to attract insects for pollination.

There are over fifty species of goldenrod in the northeast, comprising four genera, or groups marked by shared characteristics. Together, they sustain 115 species of butterflies and moths, including swallowtails, buckeyes, hairstreaks, and skippers. Some insects eat the leaves or, like the red-banded hairstreak, find nourishment in the leaf mulch. A few bird species, including chickadees, feed on the seeds. However, the big attraction is the sweet liquid nectar and powdery pollen. Monarch butterflies are particularly dependent on the high-quality goldenrod nectar during their long migration to Mexico. Along the way, they make frequent stops to power up for the next leg of the journey, and they will often travel along corridors of goldenrod. Seventeen species of bees in our area, including honeybees, bumblebees, carpenter bees, and sweat bees, depend on goldenrod for pollen or nectar, which is especially important for the queens. Instead of carrying pollen on their legs, leaf-cutter bees collect the yellow pollen on the undersides of their abdomens, making them easy to spot.

Several species of insects lay their eggs on goldenrod, causing the plant to create an astonishing new structure called a gall. When the larvae hatch, they tunnel into the plant tissue, where they spend their time munching away on the living cells. The waste and secretions of these larvae cause the cells of the host plant to multiply and enlarge, producing structures resembling tumors called galls. The galls provide both protection from the elements and additional food for the larvae without killing the goldenrod.

There are three basic types of goldenrod galls, each produced by a different insect. The most common is the ball gall, stimulated by a small fly with spotted wings called the goldenrod gall fly, which lays its tiny eggs on goldenrod stems. The eggs hatch in about ten days and the hungry larvae immediately eat their way into a stem and form a living chamber. Feeding around the clock, the larvae stimulate the host plant to create a round ball-shaped structure, giving it more space and more tasty goldenrod nutrients to feast on through the summer and fall. The larva overwinters inside the gall, producing glycerol, a type of antifreeze, which keeps the liquid cells from freezing. When the weather warms in the spring, the larva excavates an exit tunnel, stopping just short of going all the way. Then it crawls back into its cavity to pupate, emerging two weeks later as a winged adult.

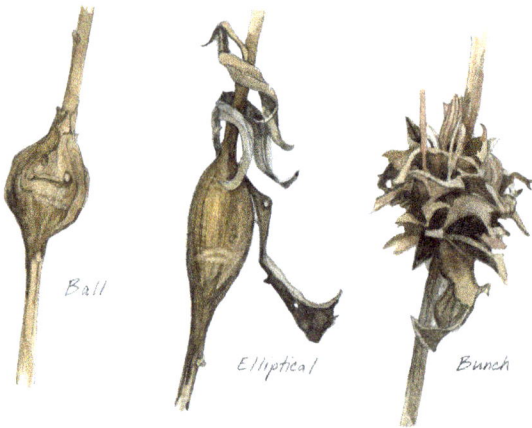

Ball

Elliptical

Bunch

The second type is the elliptical gall caused by the goldenrod gall moth. In the fall, the female lays a single egg either on a goldenrod leaf or in the leaf litter surrounding it. The egg overwinters to hatch in spring. The tiny larva crawls up an emerging plant, eating its way through the stem. This stimulates the goldenrod to form a spindle-shaped gall. The larva chews a tunnel-like escape hatch through the side of the gall plugging it with "goldenrod sawdust." Having prepared for its fall exit, the larva returns to its chamber and continues to feed and pupate inside the gall. In fall, it emerges through the escape hatch as an adult moth and flies away. The empty gall becomes available as a winter home for tiny spiders and insects.

The third type of gall, called a bunch or terminal gall, is created by the goldenrod gall midge, a small fly that lays its eggs in a leaf bud. After the larva hatches, its presence keeps the stem from growing and elongating, even though the plant continues to develop leaves. The result is a tight flower-like cluster of foliage at the top of the main stalk. Sometimes referred to as an "ecosystem engineer," the goldenrod gall midge inadvertently creates a unique habitat for spiders, insects, and other arthropods, which find food and shelter in these leaf masses.

From a distance, the wet meadow at our local park appears as a kaleidoscope of light and color, featuring purple asters, blue mist flowers, orange hawkweed, pink loosestrife, white snakeroot, and yellow goldenrod. Stepping closer, I see a lot more than pieces of the spectrum. There is a community of interdependent plants and animals supported and sustained by one another. Butterflies, bees, wasps, flies, and beetles fly from plant to plant, drinking nectar, gathering pollen, and making the most of their morning in the sun. I am reminded of the second movement of Gustav Mahler's *Symphony No. 3*, "What the Flowers in the Meadow Tell Me." This piece is light and airy, lacking the intensity of much of Mahler's music, a reflection of Mahler's feelings about the meadows around his mountain retreat. The lilting orchestration captures the ambience of a wildflower meadow, with different instruments simulating the sounds of insects fluttering and buzzing amongst the plants. In the weeks before the broadleaf trees blaze with color, our fields and wetlands sparkle with colors of their own. Like a dynamic piece of music with instruments and voices blending, the plants and insects remind us that the whole is greater than the sum of its parts.

The Great Reveal

One of the most iconic moments in film occurs in *The Wizard of Oz* after the house lands on the other side of the rainbow. As Dorothy walks out the door with her dog, Toto, the movie changes from black and white to technicolor—they aren't in Kansas anymore. I remember feeling the same way on a hike around Hathaway Pond.

It was the second time I'd visited the pond, a ten-acre kettle hole pond on Cape Cod. The first time I walked around the pond was during the winter, and I was searching for waterfowl. I was excited to find mergansers and buffleheads and paid no attention to the trees at the water's edge. When I returned on a crisp sunny day in mid-September, I didn't have any agenda. I had some extra time on my hands and happened to be in the area. It didn't occur to me that I would see some spectacular fall foliage this early in the season. To my surprise and delight, the leaves of the preeminent tree around the pond were flaming crimson, gold, orange, and purple. While taking in this vibrant display, I paged through my field guide to identify the tree.

The tupelo, *Nyssa sylvatica*, is the first tree in the northeast to change colors. Also known as black gum and sour gum, it is found from Maine to Florida and west to Minnesota, including areas of northern Texas and eastern Oklahoma. Tupelo is frequently found growing along the edges of ponds, streams, bogs, and swamps. The leaves are smooth and oval-shaped, the most commonplace of leaf designs. The generic-looking bark appears grayish brown with shallow furrows, sometimes developing thick blocky ridges on older trees. The tree can grow up to a hundred feet tall, though typically it is twenty to thirty feet high. Short, crooked branches extend horizontally from its straight, slender trunk. It is easy to walk past this tree in the winter, spring, and summer without noticing it, but not in September. Around the same time every year, the day-length timetable, or photoperiod, triggers an automatic response in this tree.

The phenomenon of photoperiod was discovered in the 1920s by two scientists who were working on crop plants. They found there were certain automatic responses in plants caused by the interplay of daylight and darkness, and these responses were independent of the weather. Later, scientists discovered that animals respond to photoperiod in a similar fashion.

Trees may appear to be standing still, yet throughout spring and summer, they are doing tremendous amounts of work. From the roots to the uppermost leaves, water is continually flowing up the tree. The roots extract water from the soil. This water is distributed throughout the tree's cell structure by means of a miniature transport system called the xylem. There is also a reverse transport system called the phloem, which carries sugars and other metabolic materials down from the leaves. Less than two percent of the water carried upward by the xylem is used by the leaves to manufacture simple sugars and build cells. The rest is released into the atmosphere. In this way, trees serve as vital links in the water cycle. A small apple orchard, containing forty trees, will release sixteen tons of water every day into the atmosphere.

As the days become shorter and summer ends, the band of cells where the leaf stem, or petiole, is attached to the twig loosens and eventually dries completely. This area of the leaf between the petiole and the twig is called the abscission zone. It is where the leaf separates from the tree, allowing the tree to conserve water during winter. The tree seals the area with a tough corky tissue that stops the flow of water into the leaf.

All summer long, leaves manufacture carbohydrates with three simple ingredients: sunlight, water, and carbon dioxide. The ingredients are mixed with chlorophyll, the pigment that makes leaves green. Chlorophyll cannot exist without water. When water stops flowing to the leaves, the chlorophyll is destroyed by the sun's rays, and we lose the dominant green color in our leaves. Other pigments, hidden all summer long by the chlorophyll, are revealed.

One of these pigments is carotin. This is the pigment that makes butter yellow and carrots orange. It is not destroyed as quickly as chlorophyll by lack of water. The bright orange sugar maples and the yellow birches, willows, and aspens expose the presence of carotin.

Another pigment, anthocyanin, is found in a variety of fruits and vegetables, including apples, plums, and beets. Anthocyanin absorbs green and blue light while reflecting red light. The brilliant red leaves on red maple, tupelo, sweetgum, and dogwood are the result of this pigment.

The light brown color of oak leaves indicates the presence of tannins. These tannins, found in the bark of the tree, are used to process animal hides, turning them a rich tan color. American beech leaves may turn either brown, yellow, or a mixture of these two colors as both tannin and carotin are present in the leaves.

Of course, not all deciduous leaves change colors. The locusts keep their chlorophyll until the leaves fall. Apparently, the corky tissues never completely seal off the leaf's supply of water. Other trees lose leaves so quickly that there isn't any time for the chlorophyll to dissipate and reveal the underlying pigments.

The weather has little effect on the timetable that trees follow for changing colors and dropping leaves. On the other hand, the intensity of fall colors is enhanced by weather conditions that are clear and crisp.

The bright reds and purples of anthocyanin are dimmed by rainy and overcast weather.

I know that many people living in the northeastern states take fall foliage for granted. Others will set out for a day of "leaf peeping" to take in the colorful displays present for only a few weeks each year. On a few occasions, when I traveled to other parts of the country, I found that I greatly missed the radiant yellows, reds, and oranges that marked the season.

One autumn, I was involved in a teaching internship in northern California. I was captivated by trees of immense size and stature, including redwood, sequoia, and Douglas fir. While there were deciduous trees, including willows, oaks, and sycamores, I missed the colors of the northeast. Another fall, I was canoeing in Florida. I traveled through swamps and meandering rivers against a glorious backdrop of stately bald cypress and live oak. Still, for me, something was missing.

The sparkling fall foliage of the northeast is remarkable, and I embrace it each year. There are laws of nature that bring about these changes. Nature's chief concern is survival. Autumn's colors and falling leaves are part of a grand and glorious arrangement to preserve deciduous trees through the winter.

The Last Wildflower

On a bleak mid-November day, I returned to the rocky outcrops on the Kittatinny Ridge of the Appalachians. I came to Hawk Mountain Sanctuary hoping to see a golden eagle or a northern goshawk, large birds of prey that often pass through Pennsylvania at the tail end of migration season. Walking the trail to North Lookout, I reflected on the how different the forest looked and felt after only three weeks between visits. A few weeks ago, the forest was ablaze in reds, yellows, oranges, and purples. Today, the dominant colors were shades of gray and brown. Though dotted with a few evergreen trees and shrubs, most of the trees were bare. The leaves had fulfilled their life's work, making food and cycling water and nutrients, and now lay lifeless in thick piles on the ground. Shuffling through them, I started thinking about their new role in the process of decomposition. I was so lost in thought that I ran into a thin, woody branch reaching into the trail. Instantly snapped out of contemplation, I realized I was looking at the buttery yellow straps of a flower—witch hazel!

It happens every year. When most of the leaves have turned and tumbled to the ground, one final wildflower makes its appearance. Witch hazel, *Hamamelis virginiana*, requires a chill below forty-five degrees Fahrenheit to open its petals. In late October and early November, before winter sets in and takes the reins, the witch hazel unveils its spidery, bright yellow flowers. As the landscape takes on an austere and barren appearance, its short, thin, strap-like petals lend color, beauty, and a pleasant fragrance to the forest.

Witch hazel is a shrub, or small tree, occasionally reaching heights of twenty or thirty feet, though typically ten to twelve feet tall. Frequently found in areas with rocky soil, several small trunks typically spring from a single root. The thickly veined leaves are round with wavy serrated edges. Flowering does not begin until the plants are at least six years old.

The branches, thick at the base, elongate to form a *V* shape. This characteristic prompted their use as divining rods for locating water underground. The ability of the wood to bend easily makes it ideal for bows and other tools, and helps explain its use for dowsing. Folklore states that a forked witch hazel branch will twist or dip when held over a unknown source of water. "Water-witching" has been practiced by diverse cultures, including Indigenous Americans, Chinese, and Europeans, presumably before they had any contact with each other. Dowsing was commonly practiced by well diggers into the twentieth century.

For centuries, witch hazel has been a popular herbal remedy. Prepared as a distilled extract made from the leaves, bark, and twigs mixed with alcohol, the astringent has been used for a wide range of medicinal purposes. Originally marketed as "golden treasure," it is approved by the Food and Drug Administration as a non-prescription drug ingredient. Most often applied to the skin and scalp, its uses include relief of inflammation, reduction of skin irritations and bleeding, the lessening of scalp sensitivity, protection from skin damage, and to treat acne. Small amounts can be ingested orally when added to herbal teas to soothe sore throats. In 1866, a Baptist minister named Thomas Dickinson opened the first commercial distillery in Essex, Connecticut, and his company is still in operation today. Over a million gallons of witch hazel extract are sold every year in this country.

Although millions of people are aware of witch hazel for its medicinal applications, few are aware of its ingenuous method for disseminating its seeds. For a full twelve months, the urn-shaped seed capsule develops a tough, durable shell resembling a double-barreled cannon. Imagine that this capsule-cannon contains two tiny cannonballs or seeds. Warmed by the sun and dried by the wind, it shrinks and splits along its sides. Enormous pressure builds to the point that the seeds are jettisoned with such force that they have been known to travel ten to twenty feet from the plant. On one occasion, an observer recorded a witch hazel seed soaring forty feet in the air. On a bright fall day, a single shrub might fire hundreds of seeds. After launching and landing, the seeds remain in the ground for up to two years where they undergo stratification, a series of warm and cold conditions, before germinating.

Naturalist and anthropologist Loren Eiseley tells the story of being awakened at night by an unfamiliar sound. Concerned that there might be an intruder, he got up to look around, only to find some small shiny black seeds on the carpet. He remembered that earlier in the day, he cut some witch hazel branches to bring inside for some fall color. Exposed to low humidity in the house, the seed capsules on the branches exploded, propelling their seeds across the room.

For years, scientists have tried to understand how witch hazel is pollinated during the cold months when most insects are inactive. While some plants are wind pollinated, witch hazel bears showy blossoms useful in attracting insects. Naturalist Berndt Heinrich discovered a group of winter moths, belonging to the owlet moth family, visiting witch hazel. The moths achieve thermoregulation by shivering, raising their body temperatures as much as fifty degrees. They fly, feed, mate, and carry pollen between plants throughout the winter months. In addition, witch hazel is pollinated by small bees, gnats, and flies that come out on warmer days.

While examining a specimen of witch hazel with a hand lens, I noticed that many leaves were rolled along the edges. After doing some research, I found this to be the work of a tortricid moth larva. The larva lives inside the leaf folds and feeds on the tissue of the inner leaves, remaining there until it emerges in spring as an adult.

There are two species of aphids that stimulate the growth of galls on the upper side of the leaves. The female cone gall aphid injects a substance into a leaf that causes it to form a miniature conical structure, resembling a witch's hat. Rich in nutrients, the gall provides food and shelter for the aphid. Another gall, resembling a tiny pineapple, is the work of the spiny witch hazel gall aphid, which lays its eggs inside a witch hazel bud.

There are many holidays that are represented by plants, including roses for Valentine's Day, shamrocks for Saint Patrick's Day, lilies at Easter, and poinsettias during the Christmas season. I nominate witch hazel for Halloween. The blooming time, the spidery petals, the dowsing mystique, and the tiny leaf galls shaped like witch hats make it the perfect candidate.

Treasure in the Dunes

There are many facets to the sandy hook of Cape Cod known as the Provincelands. Formed about five thousand years ago, it is, geologically speaking, a recent phenomenon. This new addition to the Cape Cod peninsula is the result of sand and gravel torn from the cliffs of Wellfleet and Truro that was carried northward by the rising sea. Constantly expanding and forever changing, the dunes shelter a wide variety of unique habitats shaped by the forces of wind and water. Amidst endless stretches of wind-swept sand lie swales and hollows containing red maple swamps, quaking bogs, climax forests of American beech and white oak, ghost forests, and several freshwater ponds.

The Provincelands are one of the few remaining places on Cape Cod wild and expansive enough to lose your sense of direction. Eager to explore this sandy landscape, I set off at a quick pace, marveling at the height of the dunes and examining the sparse vegetation. Wandering across sandy slopes, over ridges, and down into the hollows, I became so distracted that I lost track of where I was. While walking in a low, damp depression between dunes, trying to retrace my path, I came upon several patches of "red gold."

The Wampanoag Indians called them "ibimi," meaning bitter or sour berries, while the pilgrims called them "rubies of the bog." The early colonizers noticed a resemblance between the stamens on the flowers and the beak of a crane, thus giving the plant the name "crane-berry," which was later shortened to cranberry.

Cranberries draw little nourishment from the soil, instead they depend on air and water to supply the necessary nutrients. Like cattails and bulrushes, cranberries must grow close to fresh water, though they cannot be submerged for long periods of time. They thrive where there is enough sand available to cover their roots and vines, eliminating competition from other plants. And they depend on a moderate climate, free from heavy winds and storms. The deep, damp depressions that are scattered throughout the Provincelands dunes contain the perfect microcosms for cranberries to flourish. As I stood there admiring this wild red carpet, my mind wandered to consider the historical significance of these fruits. For hundreds of years, cranberries played an important role in American diets and culture.

In 1961, when President Kennedy designated this area a national seashore, the cranberry industry was at an all-time low. In the latter part of May, there was a killer frost which destroyed a third of the Massachusetts crop. Two years prior, the Department of Health, Education, and Welfare released information linking aminotriazole, formerly used in cranberry bogs, to cancer. In response, store owners throughout the country removed cranberry products from their shelves.

In 1930, three independent cranberry growers merged to form "Ocean Spray," the largest cranberry cooperative. Today, the company is owned by seven hundred growers in the United States, Canada, and Chile. Forty-two years earlier, in 1888, the Cape Cod Cranberry Association was formed. As one of the oldest farmer organizations in the country, they standardized measures for the sale of cranberries. Currently representing 330 cranberry growers in Massachusetts, the organization provides a unified voice to promote the cranberry industry. The professional staff conducts cranberry research, assists growers with a wide range of issues, and manages a frost warning system.

In 1887, Daniel Lumbert invented the "snap scoop," a wooden or metal box that would thread its way through the vines, picking up cranberries using a hinged lid to pull back the berries. Next came the rocker scoop, a wooden scoop with teeth. Workers placed the scoop under the vines and rocked it back and forth to gather cranberries. Before that, cranberries were harvested by hand. The workers wrapped strips of linen around their fingers to prevent them from being cut and scratched by the vines.

Cultivation of the cranberry began in 1816 when Captain Henry Hall, a Revolutionary War Veteran of Dennis, Massachusetts, realized that the wild cranberries in his bog grew better when they were covered with sand. He began transplanting cranberry vines and spreading sand over them. Before that, settlers relied solely on cranberries growing in the wild.

During the earliest days of European colonization, cranberries went seaward with every Yankee sailor. While the British sailors carried limes to ward off scurvy, Yankee sailors dined on cranberries. To protect the crop, strict laws governed the harvest of cranberries. Back in 1773, there was an ordinance in Provincetown prohibiting anyone from picking wild cranberries before the twentieth of September. Those caught disobeying this ordinance were fined the sum of one dollar and had their berries taken away.

Upon arrival to the New World, the pilgrims were presented with cranberries, a goodwill offering from the Indigenous Americans. The incorporation of cranberries as relishes, sauces, tarts, and pies into Thanksgiving celebrations has origins in this historical event. Long before the Europeans arrived in the New World, cranberries were harvested on the Cape. The Indigenous Americans mixed the berries with venison and deer fat to make "pemmican," preserving the meat for extended periods of time. Cranberries were also used medicinally and as a dye to color blankets and clothing.

Lost in the dunes among some of my favorite fruits, I don't despair. Instead, I fill my daypack with juicy ripe berries, reorient myself with the help of the sun, and hike to the top of a nearby dune. There, three mountainous dunes away, I see the roof of a dune shack. Resolving to stay on track, I set off, recalling my own family tradition. As far back as I can remember, homemade cranberry sauce was always part of our family's Thanksgiving meal. My grandmother was the first to set it on the table, followed by my mother in later years. Now, I make the cranberry sauce, and remember the treasure I found that day in the dunes.

The Fruits of November

Today is cloudy, rain-soaked, and cold. Perfect! I am off to hunt for mushrooms. Pulling on boots, grabbing my wool hat, and throwing on a jacket, I head out the door to see what I can find.

Hiking up the trail, I think back to the last time I visited these woods. Then, the trees were vibrating with color. Now, I am surrounded by subdued grays, browns, and ochers. Leafless silhouettes of maple, oak, and ash stand dormant and bare as I shuffle through leafy debris, searching for mushrooms.

When the fragile petals of flowering plants wither beneath the first frost, mushrooms remain at large, appearing in some of the most curious places. For years, I've been obsessed with them and intrigued by their capacity to pop up seemingly overnight. Pushing up through damp autumnal earth, their shapes and colors brighten otherwise bleak November days. Mushrooms festooned with purple, red, yellow, and orange caps dot the terrain. Not to be upstaged by their more colorful relatives are the shelf mushrooms. Protruding at ninety-degree angles from the sides of tree trunks and fallen trees, they lend an architectural flair to the woods.

My wife, Trudy, loves mushrooms as much as I do, though she was hesitant about eating wild ones when we first met. She had been warned, and rightly so, to eat only mushrooms found in stores or cooked at a restaurant. Since she held no expertise concerning which mushrooms were poisonous and which were not, Trudy's policy was to observe and appreciate wild mushrooms, allowing them to remain intact where they grew. On one of our first adventures together, we traveled to Nova Scotia's Kejimkujik National Park. We rented a canoe, stashed our gear in the bottom, and paddled off for a weeklong trip through the waterways. One evening, during dinner preparations, I set out to find some firewood. To my delight, I stumbled upon a large patch of chicken of the woods, *Laetiporus sulphureus*, a choice fleshy shelf mushroom that grows on the trunks of decaying and dying trees. I called Trudy over to show her what I found. We marveled at the bright yellow and orange bands of color, its rough texture, and its width. When I suggested that I was going to cook some for dinner, her response was a bit tepid. She questioned not only my identification skills but also my judgment. Why would we eat something that could potentially harm us while in such a remote location? I assured her that I was well acquainted with this mushroom and that its appearance was unique. She assured me that she would have nothing to do with it. Excitedly, I set about sautéing a batch, verbally extolling the pleasures of its texture and taste to come. Watching me out of the corner of her eye, fretting about how to best save me when I succumbed to mushroom poisoning, Trudy waited to see what would happen. Twenty minutes later, as I was packing in the rest of my dinner sans any stomach distress or convulsions, she hesitantly took a couple small bites. Trudy agreed that the mushroom was indeed delicious, and yes, it reminded her of chicken. Though just to be on the safe side, she let me finish the rest. Our trip resumed the next day, both of us paddling the sparkling lake waters in high spirits. Forty years later, we are still together; however, per her request, our mushrooms are carefully vetted. To date, we have happily eaten many delicious meals of chanterelles, morels, honey mushrooms, puffballs, and, of course, chicken of the woods.

Imagine yourself standing outside on a woodland path or even on your lawn. Below your feet, underneath the soil, are delicate, long white threads winding their way between roots and decaying vegetation. These threads are part of a giant web known as mycelium, the connective fibers of the fungal kingdom. During a large part of the year, the mycelium is invisible to all except the forester and the soil scientist. Yet, when triggered by significant rainfall, the nodes along its threads send forth fruiting bodies, or mushrooms, that burst through layers of soil and plants alike. The rapid transformation of these fruiting bodies from node to capped stem can seem almost instantaneous, offering us visible proof that the ground is alive with fungi.

An ecologist's thoughts focus on what is happening beneath the mushroom, specifically the webbing of fungal threads below the soil. Fungi are vital to the cycling of nutrients in all terrestrial ecosystems. Unlike green plants, members of the fungal kingdom do not produce leaves containing the chlorophyll necessary to make their own food. To obtain nourishment, some species of fungi form parasitic relationships, feeding from live plants. As parasites, they settle into trees weakened by disease, insect infestation, and weathering, in turn weeding the forest and keeping it healthy. Others form saprophytic relationships, living off nutrients found in dead and dying organic material, including leaves, needles, pinecones, old limbs, or rotten logs. As saprophytes, they speed up the process of decay, serving as nature's composting crew while at the same time turning decayed organic matter into nutrient-rich soil that once again nurtures new life.

Essential to the health of a forest are the mycorrhizal fungi, which have a symbiotic relationship with the roots of plants. The mycelium wraps around the rootlets of various trees and shrubs in an area, connecting them in a great web. The green plants produce simple sugars through the process of photosynthesis and supply food to the fungus. The fungi in turn assists the plants in retrieving water and nutrients, including nitrogen, phosphorous, and potassium, from the soil. This mycorrhizal webbing increases the surface area of a plant's roots, allowing the roots to take up more water and nutrients. In addition, they enable the forest trees to share nutritional resources, further protecting them from droughts, pests and soil-borne diseases. German forester and author Peter Wohlleben calls this association the "wood-wide web," while mycologist Paul Stamets refers to it as nature's neurological system.

Those who hunt mushrooms can be as curious as the mushrooms themselves. Armed with baskets, knives, and hand lenses, they roam the autumn woods in search of tasty morsels. Employing years of study and experience, they can detect mushrooms hidden beneath sand or leaves. Knowing the breadth of mycelial masses to be extensive, they will search a sizable area once they have found the first specimen. I have encountered mushroom hunters with their baskets full to the brim on days when I, an enthusiast, could hardly find one.

Serious mushroom hunters quickly learn to identify the deadly Amanitas and avoid questionable specimens. They learn to recognize the choice chanterelles, the morels, and the edible boletes, though still double check their identification skills by making a spore print and examining the powdery deposit on paper. Considering the large number of mushroom devotees in this country, there have been, thankfully, few cases of mushroom poisoning. Less than a dozen people each year make fatal mistakes. Indeed, no one wants to become a statistic. In the words of an avid mushroom collector, "There are old mushroom hunters and there are bold mushroom hunters, but there are darn few old, bold mushroom hunters."

Artists and authors may not collect mushrooms for their table, yet to them mushrooms are a source of endless fascination. There are numerous references to the world of fungi in art and literature. Among them we find mushrooms appearing as toad umbrellas, hideaways for fairies, a place for the Cheshire cat to recline, and numerous other fanciful images. Mushrooms have inspired some to combine their artistic skills with interpretation. Louis C. C. Krieger, illustrator and author of *The Mushroom Handbook*, began painting mushrooms at an early age. His artwork was so detailed and vast that he was called upon to illustrate numerous books and publications. Over time his interest in mushrooms was so keen that his art became the doorway to publishing his own interpretive work for the amateur naturalist.

I will never forget an afternoon in November when I took the fourth- and fifth-grade students in my naturalist club to the Wissahickon Gorge in Philadelphia. At the base of a dead oak tree, we found a large patch of late fall oyster mushrooms, *Sarcomyxa serotina*. Oyster mushrooms are revered for their delicate and delicious taste. The broad fan-shaped caps, the golden gills, and the white flesh make it easy to identify. Although I had eaten these before, I had never seen one in its natural setting. Now, here we were, all bending over to get a closer look at this beauty of a mushroom. What a find! Thoughts of how tasty this mushroom could be sautéed in butter with white wine flashed through my mind. Seconds later, I returned to the task at hand. This teachable moment belonged to the important role fungi play as decomposers in maintaining the health of the forest. As much as I wanted to collect a batch for dinner, I left the mushrooms in place. Sometimes, you must act like a responsible adult.

Crunch Time

Crunch. I am walking on acorns. Everywhere I look, there are hundreds covering the ground. Each step I take crushes several, knocks the caps off a few, and at times, I find myself sliding backwards. This oak-dominated forest has produced a bumper crop of acorns. Happening every few years, these mighty oaks are having a mast year.

During mast years, acorns drop from the trees in great numbers, providing ample food for squirrels, mice, deer, bears, and many species of birds. The "predator satiation" hypothesis suggests that masting years can overwhelm acorn consumers, making it possible for a greater number of acorns to survive and sprout to form new oak trees. In ensuing years, these same trees produce less. There are still lingering questions about why so many oaks simultaneously produce such an abundance of acorns.

Many variables are considered when theorizing about why oaks mast, including temperature, rainfall, drought, summer heat, and the

availability of spring winds during pollination. While the exact cause remains a mystery, the evolutionary benefit is undeniable. During a mast year, squirrels and other wildlife thrive, increasing their numbers. In intervening years, the decrease in the production of acorns limits population growth, allowing the oaks to conserve energy needed to grow new leaves and wood and replenish starches.

Fifty species of oak are found in the eastern deciduous forests, comprising sixty-eight percent of the trees. Historically, they shared their role as a keystone species with chestnuts until the chestnuts were destroyed by a fungal blight in the first half of the twentieth century. Oaks are distinguished by their bark, the shape of their leaves, and their acorns. The bark of younger oaks is smooth, while the bark on older ones is rough and thick, sometimes with deep furrows. Southern oaks, such as live oak and laurel oak, produce leaves that are long and narrow with no indentations, while the oaks in the northeast can be recognized by their distinctive lobes. Those in the white oak group have smooth rounded edges on their leaves, while the red oak group are pointy with bristly tips.

All oaks produce acorns, feeding many species of birds and mammals. The winter diet of mallards and wood ducks is comprised largely of acorns. A turkey will swallow an acorn whole, crushing the nut in its muscular gizzard. A blue jay has a tiny hook on the tip of its bill to tear open an acorn husk. Its expanded esophagus, known as a gular pouch, can hold up to five acorns. Squirrels can't consume large quantities in one sitting, so they hide and store most of their nuts for the future. It is hard to imagine that a mouse can stuff an acorn into its tiny mouth; however, they are effective hoarders known to carry small acorns in their cheek pouches. Deer swallow acorns whole and digest them easily. Bears, whose diet is eighty-five percent plants, find acorns to be a favorite food item. Both deer and bear prefer the white oak acorns, which contain less tannic acid.

I am grateful for oak trees. They provide countless benefits to the forest ecosystem as carbon capturers, oxygen suppliers, food producers, nutrient distributors, pollen and nectar providers, and much more. I am also thankful for the associations I have had with them through the years.

Each year, when the weather allows, the graduation ceremony for the seniors at my school takes place on the campus quad. There have been many years when the temperature on that day has settled into the nineties, featuring brilliant sunlight and cloudless blue skies. Fortunately, the faculty has reserved seating under the canopy of a sprawling red oak tree where we can stay cool and comfortable. I have often thanked that tree when passing by it on my way to the classroom. And I have gathered my students there on occasion to shield them from the sun.

In our backyard, there is a large pin oak tree, which provides shade when we gather with guests behind our house. When we moved here thirty years ago, it was only eight to ten feet tall, but it is now a towering tree. Before my daughter's senior high graduation party, I spent a long time trimming the lower branches so there would be lots of open space beneath this expansive tree. My efforts did not meet expectations for my mother who stood off to the side supervising my work. Laying down the pruners and heading off to my next task, I caught movement out of the corner of my eye. It was my mother, pruners in hand, moving once again around the circumference of the tree. Inspecting it from all angles, she continued to clip and shape everything I had missed.

One of my favorite trails is adjacent to the Zacharias Creek in Pennsylvania's Perkiomen Creek watershed. There is a seasoned white oak whose thick sprawling branches are riddled with woodpecker holes. I have observed five different species frequenting this august tree. What at first appears bare and lifeless provides food and housing for a variety of species.

On a canoe trip through southwest Florida, my friends and I spent many nights sleeping beneath stately live oak trees. Their broad canopy of evergreen leaves draped with Spanish moss protected us from the Floridian downpours.

Memories of bur oaks on the moist north-facing slopes of my college nature preserve stay with me to this day. They spoke to me of years spent anchoring the landscape. The bur oak, also known as the mossycup oak, features a massive trunk, deeply furrowed bark, and sizable bur-capped acorns.

Oaks support more creatures than any other tree genus in North America. In his book *The Nature of Oaks*, Douglas Tallamy, professor of Entomology and Wildlife Ecology at the University of Delaware, chronicles interactions between the mammals, birds, insects, and spiders that are found on oaks. Through painstaking research, he was able to identify hundreds of species of caterpillars in his ten-acre backyard that depend on oaks. Caterpillars are foundational in the food web, an important source of nutrition for birds and mammals, even during the winter months. Many moth species winter as caterpillars, often hiding in the crevices of bark, though sometimes found exposed on the surface of small branches. Their survival, despite harsh conditions, is due to their ability to produce glycerol. Glycerol acts much like antifreeze as it replaces water in the cells, staving off freezing temperatures and desiccation over the winter.

A curious feature of oaks is their tendency to hold on to some of their leaves throughout winter and into the early days of spring. Most of our deciduous trees lose all their leaves following the autumn color display. Oaks lose the bulk of their leaves in fall, though many remain attached. The remaining leaves rattle as the blustery winds of winter surge between them. Although the numbers of leaves diminish over winter, some remain well into spring until they are replaced by new leaves. This phenomenon is known as "marcescence."

There are many theories about how marcescence benefits a tree. One is that the presence of dead leaves makes it difficult for deer and other grazing animals to damage the tasty buds. Another theory suggests that the trees hold on to their leaves so they can produce a nutritious mulch in the spring when they need it the most. Others believe that marcescence works to block the sun on days when exposure is too intense, while some suggest that the leaves provide frost protection for the emerging buds and twigs.

Throughout history, oaks have been esteemed by cultures around the world. The Druids believed that oak trees were sacred and performed religious rituals beneath their branches. The ancient Greeks and Romans associated oaks with their sky gods, Zeus and Jupiter, respectively. Both were also known for sending bolts of lightning to the earth. Often standing taller than other trees around them, oaks are prone to lightning strikes, thus the association. Oaks are mentioned in the Bible as symbols of strength, longevity, and endurance.

There are those whose perspective on oaks does not align with mine. They complain when the trees grow tall and produce too much shade for their liking. Some have problems with the stiff leathery leaves, which take longer to decompose than those of maple or ash. Others experience annoyance with mast years, calculating the hours of work it will take to remove and dispose of hundreds of acorns.

Douglas Tallamy sees it differently, "A yard without oaks is a yard meeting only a fraction of its life-support potential." Oaks provide an abundance of ecological services. They have extensive root systems that extend horizontally from their trunks, making them ideal for soil stabilization and moisture retention. In fact, during the early years of its development, most of the growth in an oak tree occurs underground. The soil that the roots hold in place acts like a giant sponge, absorbing moisture that might otherwise erode valuable topsoil. Oaks provide shade, reduce noise pollution, improve air quality, provide habitat for wildlife, and mitigate the effects of climate change.

I am grateful for the wildlife that I see everyday thanks to the oaks. Walking along the Zacharias Creek trail, I stop to look at a bluebird perched on the branch of a white oak. Standing quiet and still, I watch a squirrel dash up the tree, stop, peer at the bird, and flick its tail while scolding the avian intruder. After the bird flies away and the squirrel continues up the tree, I move closer and notice a large spider web with fresh insects trapped inside. As I step around to see what might be on the other side, I hear it and I feel it. Crunch.

The Steward

Outside my Germantown Academy classroom in Pennsylvania, there was a wide hallway lined with expansive windows that overlooked a bird feeding station. On their way to and from my classroom, students frequently stopped to watch the birds. They liked to see which ones they could identify and if there were new birds they had never seen before. I was always eager to join them, listen to their observations, and hear what they were thinking. Often, there was an added attraction to our birdwatching—mammals! Three mammals visited regularly: gray squirrels, groundhogs, and eastern chipmunks. The students found the chipmunks the most interesting of the three. They were compact, quick, agile, and no-nonsense visitors.

Chipmunks are known for their hypervigilance. A chipmunk searching for food makes frequent abrupt stops. Scampering several feet along the trail, it halts, checks its surroundings, verifies its safety, and resumes its search. Another brief dash ends at a pile of acorns where it speedily stuffs several into already bulging cheek pouches. This stop and go pattern of movement repeats until the chipmunk slips into a nearby hole or fissure in a tree trunk.

There are twenty-four species of chipmunks in North America, with thirteen found in California, the chipmunk capital of the world. However, only one species inhabits the states east of the Rockies, *Tamias striatus*, translated as "striped steward." The Latin word *striatus* refers to the seven black and white stripes on its back. *Tamias* is in reference to its habit of dispersing nuts and seeds when collecting and storing food. The chipmunk is renowned for its ability to carry multiple seeds or nuts in its cheek pouches. Amazingly, one chipmunk can carry up to six acorns at a time.

Its cousin, the gray squirrel, randomly stashes a single acorn here and there, but the chipmunk carries multiple nuts and seeds to its burrow, ensuring sustenance through the winter months. As many as half a bushel of seeds, nuts, and other provisions have been found in a single chamber. In late summer and early fall, the chipmunk is busy carrying its provisions to its underground granary, one of the many rooms in a complex underground network that includes separate chambers for sleeping, storing food, going to the bathroom, and exiting.

Although it is easy to find the den of a fox or a groundhog, it is nearly impossible to find the subterranean home of a chipmunk. After unearthing an existing tunnel, the chipmunk digs horizontally, creating a burrow several yards long, with multiple chambers, one of which is lined with grasses for sleeping and nesting. Generally, the chipmunk makes two exits in inconspicuous places, perhaps under a log or rock. Since the exits are dug from below, there is no sign of these egresses above ground. After completing its excavation, the chipmunk plugs up the original entrance from below, spreading leaves and twigs over its hole and leaving no clue that it was ever there.

There has been a lot of debate about whether the chipmunk is a true hibernator. Hibernation comes from the Latin word *hibernatus*, which means wintering and usually refers to a torpid state in which the breathing rate, heart rate, and body temperature are greatly reduced. Woodchucks, jumping mice, and some species of bats are the only true hibernating mammals in the northeast. Black bears experience "carnivore lethargy," yet remain semi-active in their dens and even give birth to their young during the winter. A chipmunk may retire in its burrow for several weeks, waking several times during the season. It will feed from its food stashes throughout the winter and can emerge on warmer days. Some chipmunks will remain inactive for a few weeks and some for only a few days. This is referred to as partial hibernation.

The repertoire of a chipmunk is quite extensive, consisting of a wide variety of vocalizations. The familiar high-pitched chip, resembling a bird chirp, gives the chipmunk its name. Loud and clear, the sound pierces the air, at times singly, though often repeatedly. The chip trill occurs when the chipmunk is startled and when warning other chipmunks of ground predators, including raccoons, coyotes, and foxes. By contrast, when in the presence of a hawk, owl, or other aerial predator, the chipmunk makes a clucking sound, hoping to surprise and confuse the predator and provide time to escape. Both the chip and the cluck are sometimes vocalized in a rapid repeated series, creating what sounds like a trill. An additional vocalization by chipmunks is known as a chatter. This sound has been compared to that of a human voice sped up and played at a higher frequency, perhaps the inspiration for the cartoon *Alvin and the Chipmunks*. Chatter is sometimes heard during threats and fights and at times shared between a mother and her young.

Chipmunks seem to place a high value on personal hygiene. You are unlikely to find a hair out of place. They can reach all parts of their bodies with their mouths and paws. I have frequently seen them sitting on their haunches, licking their front paws and then rubbing their faces, perhaps to clean their whiskers or to wipe food away from their mouths. They are also known to take dust baths to rid themselves of mites and fleas. As a result of their diligence, they have few external parasites.

Unlike chimpanzees and wolves, chipmunks prefer living solitary lives, showing little interest in one another, except during the mating season. They live alone in their burrows and rarely interact with other chipmunks. When I've seen more than one chipmunk at our feeders, they typically ignore each other. When they do interact, it is usually with threatening postures or minor brawls. I have never seen any indication that they are looking for social engagement. Most of their waking hours, they seem preoccupied with finding food. Although chipmunks feed primarily on nuts, seeds, mushrooms, and berries, they supplement their diet with frogs, salamanders, mice, insects, small birds, and occasionally bird eggs and nestlings.

Chipmunks spend most of their lives roaming the grounds of forests, meadows, and the edges in-between, still they climb trees to reach tasty acorns or to escape from predators. They rarely climb very high, as their delicate claws are not ideal for gripping and their bodies and legs are not well-adapted for leaping between branches.

On a recent visit to Militia Hill Hawk Watch, I spent more time watching chipmunks than observing raptors. Despite the promising weather forecast, the only raptors present were a group of resident turkey vultures soaring in their characteristic dihedral flight pattern. I turned my attention to the bird feeding station near the tower. There were chipmunks scampering around the feeders, patrolling the ground for seeds. At least five individuals intermittently searched the area, though never more than two at a time. During my observation I watched a chipmunk make a quick dash to dig through the seeds that had fallen on the ground. It picked up one seed at a time, pushing each one into its bulging cheek pouches. Another climbed onto a stump, checked its surroundings, and retrieved a few seeds, then dashed back to the ground. At times, I would observe a chipmunk nibbling and gnawing on a branch. There were several instances of chipmunks chasing one another and one tiny brawl involving two chipmunks somersaulting over one another. Despite the scarcity of raptors, there were other creatures to observe while standing on the hawk watch platform. I watched my fellow hawk watchers leave in disappointment, but I felt lucky to peer into the lives of chipmunks as they prepare for winter.

Night Screamer

What was that? My eyes flew open as I sat up straight. I bolted out of bed, opened the window, and scanned the area. Seconds later, I heard it again, an ear-piercing, otherworldly shriek that seemed to be right next to the house. Twenty minutes later, unable to get back to sleep, I decided to go downstairs and do some research. To my surprise, I found that this screaming cry came from a red fox.

Although they communicate primarily through scent and make noise only on rare occasions, scientists have identified forty distinct vocalizations made by foxes, including clicks, barks, growls, laughs, chatters, and screams. These sounds may be used to locate a family member, mark territory, attract a mate, achieve social dominance, or warn a potential predator. Vocalizations are easily heard during late fall and winter due to the lack of vegetation to buffer sound.

There are two species of foxes in the northeast. The native gray fox, *Urocyon cinereoargenteus*, prefers dense woods with rocky ledges. The common red fox, *Vulpes vulpes*, is found around the edges of forested areas and open fields, including suburban areas bordered by small forest

fragments. Considered the most widely distributed carnivorous land mammal in the world, the red fox is found across all of Europe, some parts of Russia, Japan, India, northern Africa, and Australia, along with the Americas. Genetic evidence places the ancestors of the red fox in the Middle East four hundred thousand years ago before moving into Eurasia, on to Siberia, and eventually across the land bridge between Russia and Alaska. Once in western North America, the red fox became a resident of the northern latitudes and mountain regions. The red fox was not found in eastern North America until the mid-1800s, when aristocrats brought it here from Europe for the sport of fox hunting. Its intelligence, tenacity, and flexible diet enabled the fox to adapt easily to the region. Small mammals, birds, amphibians, and insects, along with berries and other fruits, were plentiful in the northeast.

Although foxes are occasionally attacked by eagles and coyotes, they have few natural predators. Habitat destruction, vehicular traffic, and trapping are the most significant threats to their survival. They are, however, susceptible to mange, a skin disease caused by tiny sarcoptic mites less than a quarter inch long. Thousands may burrow through the skin, causing severe itching, hair loss, the formation of scabs and lesions, and sometimes death from infection.

There are few animals as common in folklore around the world as the fox. Frequently depicted as sneaky and quick-witted, they are also portrayed as wise transcendent spirits. Many Indigenous American myths depict the fox as a trickster companion to the coyote. In Celtic mythology, the fox is a shapeshifter that can switch between canine and human forms. Chinese folklore pictures the fox as a magical being with paranormal abilities. Depending on the story, the fox can be a benevolent guardian who guides humans in times of need or a wily scoundrel causing mischief and harm.

A member of the dog family, foxes are closely related to wolves and coyotes. However, in many ways, the behavior of a fox is more like a cat than a dog. Like cats, they walk on their toes, making them speedy and silent. You will never find other members of the dog family in a tree, yet the gray fox is an excellent tree climber. The red fox doesn't possess this skill, though it may jump high and leap from branch to branch.

While dogs tend to meander from scent to scent, foxes and cats walk in a straight line with each back foot overlapping the front of a previous step. Similar to cats, foxes are nocturnal, with vertically slanted pupils to increase visibility in dim light and to help them judge the distance of their prey. Foxes use the whiskers on their long sensitive snouts to navigate and will stalk their prey like a cat, crouching low to the ground, digging in the soil, and pouncing on an unsuspecting rabbit or rodent.

Some of the best athletes in the animal kingdom, foxes can run up to thirty-one miles per hour, jump over six-foot high fences, and swim across a river or lake. Foxes are known for the way they ambush their prey by leaping into the air and landing on their target. Their large ears provide exceptional hearing, which allows them to pinpoint sound with great accuracy. Studies suggest that they align their pounces to the earth's magnetic field. It is believed that a protein in their eyes causes a shadow when it is aligned with the earth's magnetic field. Scientists found that foxes successfully pounce on their prey seventy-four percent of the time when they align to the north. Many animals have a magnetic sense, including migrating birds and many species of insects, but only the fox uses it to judge distance, direction, and depth.

Foxes develop a thick winter coat and remain active throughout the winter months. They continue to hunt and forage, and dens are used only during mating season. It is not unusual to find a fox sleeping in the open with its long, insulated tail wrapped around its body, sometimes beneath a blanket of freshly fallen snow. Foxes are solitary, except when they are raising their young in their dens.

Breeding season begins in February. Foxes construct their dens on a hillside, often at the edge of the woods. Two pairs of foxes may share a burrow, which can be used for several generations. The tunnels measure three to ten feet in length, with at least two means of egress. Like skunks, foxes have a musty smell that comes from the glands at the base of their tails. This scent is powerful and can be detected when near a fox den.

Fox kits are born in early spring and remain in their den with their mother while the father hunts for food. After four or five weeks, they emerge in the open, and when seven months old, the pups are ready to go off on their own. As youngsters, they possess little fear of humans and can often be easily spotted in an open field or yard. I've had the good fortune to observe the pups playing on several occasions. Full of energy, they jump in the air, pounce on each other, and wrestle for dominance. I've seen two pups standing on their hind legs while each one tries to push the other backwards.

Now that I recognize the scream of the red fox, it doesn't scare me like it did that night. In fact, I like hearing the sound. Lying comfortably in bed at night, I enjoy hearing its voice. I am reminded that despite all the development in our area, there remains a vestige of wildness nearby.

Squid Pro Quo

"All along the strip of wet sand that marks the ebbing and
flowing of the tide, death walks hugely and in many forms."
–Loren Eiseley

It was a tough week for squid. The beach on the outer shore of Cape
Cod was littered with squid cast ashore by the stormy sea. Walking
along Nauset Beach in Orleans on an evening in late November, I found
hundreds piled up on the sand, unable to make it back to the water. What
happened? Was it the unusually high tides, cooling temperatures, intense
winds, or pursuit by predators that resulted in this mass stranding?

Low tide often reveals a variety
of marine creatures no longer
swimming, diving, pulsating, or
walking. Whether they are missing
vital body parts or even intact, it was
usually obvious to me that their lives
had ended. On this day, as I walked
closer to the squid, I assumed they
were all dead. Lying motionless on
the sand, they appeared lifeless. I
picked one up and noticed a slight
movement in some of the tentacles.
The tiny red and purple dots covering
the skin were randomly pulsing. I
picked up a few more squid and took
them down to the water, hoping it
was not too late to help them recover. Sadly, in seconds, they all sank to
the bottom. Scanning the beach, I retrieved a plastic bag from its sandy
snare. Into the bag I placed a few dead squid to take to my classes. At
least I could turn this mass stranding into an engaging lab activity to
teach students about the unique physiology of squid.

Squid are part of a large phylum of soft-bodied organisms called
mollusks. Most mollusks, like clams, mussels, oysters, and snails, have

hard outer shells, but the squid has a flexible internal shell much like a backbone, called the pen. As an anatomical reminder, following our dissection, my students use the pen to write their names in squid ink.

Without the protection of a hard shell, the squid has developed unique adaptations for staying clear of predators. It can dart back and forth at record-breaking speeds or disappear into the background. Squirting an inky fluid into the water, it can create a smoke screen, hiding its movements and confusing its enemies. And it can suddenly appear bigger by shooting out its tentacles.

In place of the muscular foot of a snail or clam, the squid has ten arms, or tentacles, attached to its head. This classifies the squid, along with the octopus and cuttlefish, as a "cephalopod," which means head footed. The two longer arms are used for capturing fish and crustaceans, while the shorter arms hold the food as the squid eats. Its mouth resembles a hard parrot-like beak, which it uses for ripping food into small pieces.

The squid has two large image-perceiving eyes, remarkably like the human eye in construction. It has a well-developed nervous system and an unusually large brain in relation to its size. Many species of squid are highly social and use various forms of communication. The squid and the octopus are the most highly evolved and intelligent species of invertebrates.

Covering the body of the squid like a loose coat is the mantle. When the mantle is relaxed, water enters through a small tube called the funnel. Squid move rapidly by contracting the mantle to suck in a quantity of water, then squirting it out through the funnel. Thus, a squid propels itself in the direction of its choice. By changing the angle of the funnel, it can move forwards, backwards, sideways, or up and down. When threatened, the squid can dart off, deploying one squirt within five hundredths of a second. The squid's streamlined shape is ideal for slicing through the water. Its flat rear fin serves as a rudder, while the side fins are used for hovering or when slow movements are needed. Its ten tentacles, pressed together, act as a steering device. Contrary to most mollusks who move at an exceedingly slow pace, squid move with astounding speed and agility.

Among its many adaptations, squid can change colors seemingly in an instant. Its body is covered with cells called chromatophores. Inside these cells are tiny transparent sacs containing pigments which may be brown, red, yellow, black, or orange. A complex system of muscles and nerves attaches to each sac, controlling expansion and contraction. When the sacs are expanded, more color is seen. Once the sacs contract and relax, the color dims. Two other types of cells, leucophores and iridophores, also assist the squid in its camouflaging color changes. Leucophores act like tiny mirrors, reflecting the light that surrounds the squid, while iridophores produce iridescent greens, silvers, blues, and golds.

The Norwegian explorer Thor Heyerdahl noted that certain species of squid could take to the air. When aboard the Kon-Tiki, he observed large groups of squid propel themselves out of the water and, like flying fish, sail as much as fifty feet through the air. Sometimes they leapt so high that they landed on the decks of ships. To date, scientists believe that there are numerous flying squid species, many of which have yet to be discovered. Among them is the arrow squid, which have been spotted leaping approximately ten feet above the surface of the water and undulating their fins to reach distances approaching one hundred feet. Explanations for this behavior include the need to escape from predators.

Perhaps the most astonishing species is the giant squid. Living at depths two thousand feet below sea level, their appearance and size has given rise to many of our sea monster stories. Measuring some fifty feet in length, it is a favorite food of sperm whales. Apparently, the squid does not surrender its life easily, as numerous scars created by the suckers along its tentacles are seen on the bodies of the whales. The giant squid's indigestible horny beak lodges in the sperm whale's intestines, where it is coated with a waxy secretion called ambergris. This is the same substance once used to make expensive perfumes.

The hundreds of squid I found washed ashore that morning were the northern shortfin squid, *Illex illecebrosus*, a common migratory species found throughout the northwestern Atlantic from the coast of Maine to Florida. They usually inhabit deeper waters. Perhaps they entered the shallows to chase young mackerel or to flee from striped bass, dolphins, porpoises, or seals. Perhaps the sudden cooling of the water chilled the squid to the point of insensibility, causing them to drift ashore.

I walk the November beach eager to see what the high tide has left behind. My excitement is laced with a sense of foreboding. Last week, there were squid by the hundreds. What has the tide left behind today?

White Lightning

There are many rewards that come to the birder who walks along our wave-beaten coast. During the warmer months, there are a wide variety of shorebirds, including gulls, terns, sandpipers, and plovers, feasting at the edge of a tideline or synchronously flying wingtip to wingtip as if they are a single organism. In late fall and winter, several species of sea ducks, such as scoters and eiders, float the ocean's rolling swells, looking much like surfers waiting to catch a wave. If you're lucky, it's possible to see the silhouette of a large, streamlined bird approach. Perhaps searching for its next meal, it glides low over the water and flies out of sight as quickly as it arrived. A master of the wind, the northern gannet combines powerful wing strokes with prolonged glides.

The largest seabird found in the waters of the North Atlantic, an adult northern gannet, *Morus bassanus*, has a wingspan approaching six feet. When plunging into the water, it tucks its wings close to its body resembling an arrow. The snow-white body, black-tipped wings, thick spear-like pale blue bill, and golden crown belong to the gannet alone. Its closest relative, the booby, is found in the warmer waters of the southern Atlantic. Weighing five to eight pounds, the gannet is the heavyweight among the plunge-diving birds, a category which includes kingfishers and terns.

My first encounter with these magnificent birds occurred one day in late October. I was on a whale watch boat heading out to Stellwagen Bank off the coast of Massachusetts. It was a crisp, clear day, enabling us to see miles into the distance—perfect for viewing whales. Approximately an hour into the trip, spouts were spotted on all sides of the boat. Over the course of a three-hour period, twenty finback whales had been seen. Ever-present seabird sightings added to the excitement of the day. Gulls, terns, shearwaters, and gannets appeared in great numbers. They were all here for the same thing. Thousands of sand lance, a primary food source for whales and sea birds, were devoured that day.

My memories of the gannets, their speed, form, and behavior, are vivid to this day. They flew in from all directions around us, diving off the bow, behind the stern, to the port and starboard of the boat. As with the sighting of each whale, when we sighted a gannet, everyone ran to get a good look. The gannets dove so close to one another that we were sure some of them would collide under water. It is hard to believe there weren't any casualties. Fortunately, their keen eyesight and constant vocalizations keeps them clear of other birds.

The athleticism of these skillful divers is impressive. Diving from heights some one hundred feet in the air, a gannet plummets headfirst into the waves. Just before piercing the surface of the water, the bird folds its wings along the sides of its body, creating a sleek, streamlined shape resembling an arrow. At the same time, it draws a protective membrane over its eyes and inflates organs in the neck and chest, which cushion the body upon impact. Just before it hits the ocean surface, the neck muscles lock each vertebra in place. To prevent water from entering its nasal cavity during these high-speed dives, a gannet

can close the opening in its beak. Traveling at speeds up to sixty feet per second, it pierces the water, attaining depths up to seventy-two feet, absorbing the impact with its hard protective skull and cushioning air sacs. Instantly, the gannet adapts its eyes for underwater vision, using its wings and feet to propel itself deeper underwater. After catching a fish, the gannet inflates tiny airbags under the skin to return to the surface, where it will become airborne once more.

Remarkably, gannets emerge from the water completely dry. The complex interlocking structure of each outer feather serves as a barrier to the penetration of sea water. In addition, they constantly waterproof their dense feathers with a waxy substance secreted by the oil glands at the base of their tails. They use their beaks to collect the secretion, then carefully apply it to each outer feather. The result is much like rain rolling off the roof of a freshly waxed car.

Gannets spend most of their lives out at sea, coming ashore only to breed. On long migratory flights, half of the brain dozes off at time, enabling them to sleep while in flight. Northern gannets can regularly be seen along the Atlantic and Gulf coasts from Maine to Texas, except during the summer months. The best time to look for them is during their spring and fall migrations, although they are often seen from shore during the winter months. In North America, they breed in six large colonies, three in the Gulf of St. Lawrence and three in the North Atlantic off the coasts of Labrador and Newfoundland. Slow and awkward on land, they nest high on steep rocky cliffs. Here they can take advantage of strong sea winds that are forced upward when hitting the rocks. Spreading their long, slender wings, they catch the air currents, which lift them skyward. The largest colony is on the island of Bonaventure, adjacent to Quebec's Gaspé Peninsula, where its two-hundred-fifty-foot cliffs boast an estimated fifty-five thousand pairs. Interestingly, this number represents only half of a once thriving population observed in the 1800s. When John James Audubon sailed into the area in 1833, he recorded an estimated population of over one hundred thousand pairs. By the early 1900s, the population of northern gannets had been decimated to near extinction. In the eleventh hour, the Canadian government moved to protect all the nesting sea birds on the islands of the Gaspé Peninsula.

On his voyage to record bird populations in the North Atlantic, Audubon shed light on their demise. He described the fate met by thousands of gannets in his diaries. Notable are passages detailing frequent visits by Labrador fishermen who beat the nesting gannets with clubs, creating a frenzy of panicked birds. During at least one such intrusion, over five hundred birds had been killed by six men in an hour. The birds were skinned, their flesh cut off in chunks and sold as codfish bait to the local fishermen.

When ornithologist Arthur Cleveland Bent visited Bonaventure in 1904, the number of gannets totaled less than three thousand birds. During a subsequent visit to the islands off the Labrador coast north of the peninsula, he reflected upon the complete absence of gannets. Fortunately, in the nick of time, the Bonaventure Island and Percé Rock Migratory Bird Sanctuary was established by the Canadian government in 1919, and the gannet population has been increasing ever since. Still, gannets are vulnerable to a variety of issues affecting all seabirds, including toxic contaminants, plastics, mounting levels of trash, fishing nets, overfishing, and climate change.

Like their relatives, the boobies, gannets mate for life. Each year, they renew their bonds at the nest site within the colony, referred to as a gannetry. Nests are compact masses of seaweeds, land plants, and debris, usually collected by the male. The female lays a single pale blue to white egg, which takes forty-two to forty-six days to hatch. Both male and female care for and feed the young. They separate when their chick leaves the nest to reunite again the following spring, locating each other amongst thousands of adult and juvenile gannets. It remains a mystery as to how they find their mates. When greeting each other, they may shake their heads back and forth, bow, call, or engage in "bill fencing." Many nature photographers have captured the striking image of a nesting pair of gannets with their necks outstretched, beaks crossed and pointed skyward.

Long before I saw my first gannet, I was introduced to this intriguing bird in my tenth-grade English class. In Homer's *Odyssey*, the sea goddess Leucothea, also known as the Goddess of Sailors, appears in the likeness of a gannet. She offers the shipwrecked Odysseus her veil, telling him to leave his raft behind, shed his clothes, and wind the veil around himself. Thus, Odysseus safely reaches dry land to continue his journey.

Whether soaring in the updrafts, plunging headfirst into frothy seas, or rocketing underwater, gannets are champions of the marine environment. Walking the beach on a cold windy morning, I am captivated by the agile maneuvers of a gannet. I am grateful to share this moment with such an awe-inspiring bird.

The First Snow

"And to think it all started with one flake."
–Bil Keane, cartoonist

I could feel it coming last night. Now in the early hours of the morning, I was eager to check. Slipping out of my warm bed, I got up and walked to the closest window. Pushing the curtains aside, I saw it. The first snow of the season had fallen. Abandoning any normal morning routines, I threw on some clothes and charged outside to investigate.

Tiny white "flowers" tumbled down on my coat sleeves. I paused to examine the snow crystals with my hand lens. I am reminded that no two crystals are identical. Meteorologists classify a few basic types of crystal formations based on the temperature and the humidity present in the air when the crystals develop. Small column-shaped crystals are formed when the air is cold and little moisture is present, while stellar or star-shaped crystals occur when there is increased moisture in the air and the temperature is higher. On their journey earthwards, crystals often pass through a range of conditions prior to their soft landing.

Wilson "Snowflake" Bentley was so obsessed by snow that he devoted his life to studying snow crystals. In 1880, this Vermont farm boy was given a microscope for his fifteenth birthday. From that moment on, he spent his winters capturing snowflakes on film with his microscope and camera. During his lifetime, he took over 5,000 photographs of snow crystals, and 2,500 of these microphotographs can be seen in his book *Snow Crystals*, published in 1931. When I was first introduced to his book, I thought I was looking at paintings and had no idea the pictures were actual photographs.

Snow crystals form in clouds when the temperature is between thirty-two and minus thirty-nine degrees Fahrenheit. These clouds are made up of billions of microscopic water droplets along with particles of dust and pollen. These water droplets adhere to the particulates, forming ice crystals. The crystals change and grow as they descend through layers of atmospheric temperature changes. While falling, some crystals merge, others break apart to form the nucleus of a new crystal. This process repeats numerous times to create the snowflakes we see and the snowstorms we experience. The crystalline structure of snowflakes makes them translucent. Therefore, when light shines on a snowflake, the light is bent and scattered, which results in our perception of white light. Highly compacted and layered snows can have a bluish appearance due to the lack of air between crystals. In this case, visible light on the red spectrum is absorbed. Snow can also appear blue if there is a layer of meltwater that is reflecting blue sky.

This morning, there are close to four inches of snow on the ground, just enough to make things interesting. It has transformed some of the neighborhood's most manicured yards into storybook illustrations. Even the tiny grove of pitch pine and scrub oak behind my house takes on the veneer of an enchanted forest.

Freshly fallen snow covering woodland trails and roadways offers me an opportune glimpse into the private lives of our resident wildlife. I follow the tracks of a cottontail rabbit, stopping at several small shrubs where there is evidence of its appetite for dormant buds and twigs. Each twig is cleanly cut at a forty-five-degree angle. As I continue to follow its loping gait, I notice that the snow beneath a larger bush has been packed down by the weight of its resting body. Perhaps it was taking cover to escape detection by another hungry winter resident. Certainly, its light brown coloration provides the necessary camouflage.

Rabbit tracks appear oval with only four of the five toes visible in the snow. Their tracks show that their back legs must overtake their front in a single movement. Rabbits stretch their two smaller paws ahead, elongating the body, then instantly place the rear feet to the sides of the front paws propelling it forward. When startled and during courtship, rabbits jump and twist in the air, all four paws off the ground. They land with back legs stretched out behind the body and front legs reaching forward. Every now and then along the trail, they leave behind a scattering of small, compressed pellets of leaf and twig detritus. Rabbits keep no secrets.

Squirrels will also gallop through woods, fields, and backyard lawns. Their tracks appear similar, though much smaller than those of rabbits, and they always place their front feet side-by-side. I noticed a row of squirrel tracks leading from one tree to the next and back again. In a few places, the squirrel stopped to dig in the snow, perhaps searching for acorns. They are busy little creatures, and even major snowstorms don't seem to slow them down. Compared to a rabbit's wandering nature, squirrels move in fits and starts, constantly searching for food and dodging danger. When stripping a pine or spruce cone, they eat or store the seeds, leaving the leftover woody scales in a pile commonly called a midden. Squirrel middens can also be composed of acorn or walnut husks.

Near my back door I saw some tiny tracks leading to a small tunnel entrance. I am guessing these tracks belong to a mouse on the prowl for something good to eat. This early morning snowfall has provided an effective escape route so that it can move through a series of tunnels instead of along open ground. However, there are still those predators, such as foxes and coyotes, who rely less on sight and more on sound for dining in a snowstorm.

My hunger mounting, I headed back to the house to get a quick breakfast. On the way, I ran into a woman walking her dog. She was clearly not dressed for the occasion and looked miserable. "Beautiful day," I remarked as we passed. The woman shook her head and laughed. She thought I was kidding. To some people, snow is an inconvenience; to others, like me, it renews our sense of wonder.

Among the Evergreens

Every year, during the final weeks of December, many of us bring the great outdoors indoors for a few weeks. Our homes and places of work are adorned with the greens of the natural world. The pines, spruces, firs, and cedars take on new meaning and prominence.

When I am in the presence of evergreens, my mind begins to wander. As a child, I felt a special connection to the towering white pine, *Pinus strobus*, in our front yard. Easily occupying half the front lawn, it shed layers of pine needles, which formed a soft, thick mulch at the base of its trunk. Best of all, its sturdy, evenly spaced branches made the pine easy to climb. Often my friends would join me because I had the best climbing tree in the neighborhood. And there were many days when it was just me, sitting with my back against the trunk, daydreaming in my tree.

In my early twenties I lived and worked on Cape Cod, where pine/oak forests comprise most of the interior section of this sandy peninsula. Named for the high resin content in its wood, pitch pine, *Pinus rigida*, adapts well to sandy soil on the Atlantic shoreline and alongside the Great Lakes. Their crooked trunks and asymmetrical branches make them look like they belong in a fairytale. Walking through these forests was a sensual experience. Ocean breezes wafted through the branches, stirring up the aromatic smells of pine and earth. The sound of ascending chromatic scales revealed the presence of a prairie warbler.

For twenty-five years, I spent a portion of my summer living on an island in Maine. I have a special place in my heart for the rocky shore and the cathedral-like forests of spruce and fir that cover the island. Red spruce, *Picea rubens*, and white spruce, *Picea glauca*, anchor the forest ecosystem, accompanied by balsam fir, *Abies balsamea*. Walking amongst the spruce and fir on a foggy day transported me to a primordial era, especially when the squawk of a great blue heron echoed through the trees from the intertidal zone. Ambling farther down the needle-laden trails, I might hear the rising trill of a parula warbler, the ethereal flute-like sound of a hermit thrush, or the "zee zee zee zoo zee" of a black-throated green warbler.

In ancient deposits of coal and shale, we see remains of modern-day conifers, as these distinguished members of the plant kingdom preceded the dinosaurs. I imagine what the world must have been like 310 million years ago when conifers first originated in Europe and North America. There were no flowering plants, nectar-gathering insects, birds, or mammals. The earth was dappled with shades of green, minus the colors of fruits and flowers. Species have arrived and departed. Ice has engulfed and scoured the landscape many times over. Yet the conifers remain to this day, adapting to meet their needs in an ever-changing world.

Back when the giant horsetails and tree ferns were sending their spores to the wind, the plant kingdom came up with a new idea that changed the face of the planet. The conifers were some of the earliest plants to successfully reproduce by means of a new evolutionary device, the seed.

Long before the advent of fruits, nuts, and berries, the seeds of this ancient race lie naked along the scales of hard woody cones, hence the name "conifer." The scales spiral upwards, providing openings for wind-blown pollen to settle inside the scales.

Unlike modern trees, conifers feature a singular trunk from its base to the top without forking. The branches are arranged in evenly spaced whorls around the trunk, and the age of the tree can be estimated by the number of whorls. The shallow root system spreads horizontally beneath the soil. The seedlings are hard and woody, unlike those of the tender deciduous trees. A strong-smelling sticky sap courses through the veins of the wood, protecting the tree from invasions of insects and fungi.

The needles of North American conifers appear in a few basic arrangements. They vary in texture from the soft and delicate ones on the white pine to the short, pointed needles on many spruces. Pine needles are attached to the branches in clusters called fascicles. Typically, there are two, three, or five needles to a cluster. Sharply pointed spruce needles are arranged in an alternate pattern around the twigs. Soft and flat, fir needles lay horizontally along their branches.

While deciduous trees lose their leaves in the fall and acquire new ones in the spring, the evergreens lose and gain their leaves constantly through the year. Superficially, they appear to be "evergreen" regardless of the season, but there are always live and dead needles present. In the words of author Aldo Leopold in *A Sand County Almanac*: "Plants have earned the reputation of being evergreen by the same device that governments use to achieve the appearance of perpetuity, overlapping terms of office. By taking on new needles on the new growth of each year and discarding old needles at longer intervals, they have led the casual onlooker to believe that needles remain forever."

These needle-shaped leaves, infused with resin and a waterproof wax, protect the tree from harsh weather conditions, including high winds, snow, ice, and rain. They are designed to conserve water and, for the most part, are unaffected by extremes in temperature. Hence, we find evergreen forests in frigid northern climes and in the oppressively hot southern regions. Wherever there is enough earth to cover their roots, an evergreen forest can establish a foothold. A forest of Scotch pine,

Pinus sylvestris, grows in Siberia, where temperatures hover around fifty below for most of the winter months.

In places suffering from drought conditions, the needle-leaf has the unique ability to absorb traces of moisture from the air. Water passes down the tree and into the roots. Thus, we see spruce and fir growing on the edge of mountainsides, junipers in the desert, and pines along the sandy shores of Cape Cod and the New Jersey pine barrens.

In areas subject to frequent fire, the conifers have, once again, proven their adaptability. The cones of lodgepole, *Pinus contorta*, knobcone, *Pinus attenuata*, pitch, *Pinus rigida*, and Jack pine, *Pinus banksiana*, open when heated. Older, diseased trees may be destroyed by fire; however, the intense heat opens the cones and disperses the seeds.

Long before the first Christmas, the custom of decorating the home by bringing evergreens indoors added a festive flair to the celebration of the winter solstice. The tradition was practiced by many cultures, including the ancient Egyptians, the Romans, the Druids, and the Vikings. When daylight was at an all-time low, the greens reminded them that nature was still alive and well. Each year, as we celebrate the Yuletide season, the evergreens keep us connected to the natural world. During the bleakest days of winter, they remind us that new life and new growth are just around the corner.

Appendix

Community Science - Arachnid Explorations

by Ron Smith

Over the past two decades, I have had the opportunity to lead and participate in a variety of community science initiatives. Some of these include monitoring migratory shorebird populations along the mid-Atlantic seaboard, rescuing stranded and trapped horseshoe crabs on the beaches of Delaware Bay, documenting amphibian communities in hidden ephemeral pools of the New Jersey Pine Barrens, and recovering otherwise doomed sea turtle eggs from nests below the high tide line. I have shared remarkable moments of conservation stewardship with teams of students, colleagues and friends. All these projects involved regionally and globally significant species with high priority and high-profile conservation stories. The species are often well known to many, and the data collected by our efforts has supported specific goals central to the work of the conservation community.

Still, the story of global biodiversity decline remains incomplete at best. There are countless species and communities in trouble, often in very surprising locations. If we do not take the time to establish the baseline data applicable to their conservation status, we will not have the best opportunity to evaluate them and, if needed, rally others to the call for their protection. When we consider conservation hotspots, we focus on habitats harboring species that are clearly threatened. Habitat loss and fragmentation and climate change have become ever-present threats to the recovery of species. Not only must we become active participants in the monitoring of imperiled plants and animals, we need to take steps in our own neighborhoods and gardens to support habitat and the overall health of our backyard biodiversity.

I recently tasked my students with documenting invertebrate diversity in gardens. Some of the gardens they visited had been amended with significant applications of synthetic fertilizers and pesticides. When we compared the data collected from the treated gardens to that collected from gardens cultivated without soil and plot amendments, the results were definitive. Gardens tended without the use of chemical inputs supported greater species abundance and diversity. Perhaps most notable in the data was the abundance of spiders present in the untreated gardens compared to their near absence in the biological deserts of sod grass and crushed rock gardens.

Spiders are present in a variety of habitats and, on the home front, occupy virtually every space in our homes and gardens. Consider for a moment the many pesky invertebrates that can cause problems for people—house flies, termites, mosquitoes, fruit flies and ants can all be unwelcome visitors to our kitchen cabinets and picnic tables. Want a sustainable approach to keeping them in check? Encourage and support the presence of spiders. As predators, spiders can snag and ambush virtually any other type of garden invertebrate. This essential ecosystem service keeps the balance in our backyard ecosystems.

Occupying diverse habitats around the home—in woodpiles, along fences and hedgerows, in the tall vegetation of our garden beds and between the twigs of our shrubs and trees—spiders can be found almost everywhere we look. Building webs, camouflaged against flower petals and occupying tree cavities, they quietly help keep the invertebrate community in balance.

Few projects have been established to explore, document, and protect spider communities. This creates the ideal opportunity for community scientists. Having initiated projects in my own garden, in the local county park and as educational initiatives for teacher field training programs, I have found spider studies an accessible and enjoyable opportunity for every nature enthusiast. Whether sweep netting or setting pitfall traps, spiders can be observed up close using simple methods and minimal equipment. Online resources and field guides can be used to make identifications, and partnerships with conservation groups can expand your efforts and bring together community members.

Over the past two years, our Earth Day Fair has featured spider exhibits with the intent of increasing interest in and awareness about protecting these invertebrate predators. Terraria containing a variety of local species, collected during our community science sampling, are on temporary display. There are interactive games highlighting spider biology and ecology and invitations to participate in field experiences.

Spiders qualify as an umbrella species. When successful conservation measures are put in place for them, these same measures result in the protection of other species within their proximity. Habitat diversity in natural settings—backyards, meadows and woodlands—must be protected to secure spider populations. Landscape practices employed in gardens must include considerations for invertebrate conservation. Avoiding pesticides and herbicides, maintaining natural spaces, and increasing habitat diversity will benefit spider species. Assessing spider diversity, and creating and monitoring spider habitat are fundamental to community science endeavors.

Assessing the efficacy of habitat protection and garden management for spider communities can reveal which efforts are most beneficial. Our latest garden conservation project—Leave the Leaves (an initiative of the Invertebrate Conservation Organization Xerces Society)—will benefit spiders and various other invertebrates in our backyards and gardens. Our spring initiative is to examine the abundance and richness of spiders that have benefited from this simple conservation action.

Spiders are one of many easily overlooked invertebrate groups that can quietly disappear in the habitats they occupy. They are surprisingly accessible, amazingly beautiful and so very important for the ecosystem services they provide. It's time to bring them to the forefront of conservation efforts, and community science is the perfect way to make this happen.

This past fall, as I sat in the back garden on a cool morning I observed the surprisingly diverse habitat of our urban plot. Next to me, a Carolina wren was carefully watching the staccato movements of a jumping spider. I observed the wren following the movements of the arachnid and was delighted that the spider dropped onto the wooden seat that it now shared with me. The wren flew off and the spider seemed to briefly enjoy my company before scrambling under the seat where I sat. Grateful for the brief encounter, I wished her well and contemplated my next arachnid adventure.

Acknowledgments

Each plant or animals within these pages was chosen based on a personal memorable experience. While there are many other species that evoke the fall season, these are the ones that have touched my life directly. I was alone for several of these encounters, though more often with my wife, friends, students, or colleagues. It has been said that "a pleasure shared is a pleasure doubled." I heartily agree.

I am especially grateful to my talented wife, Trudy Phillips, who shared many of the experiences in this book with me. She was with me every step of the way, from discussing and shaping the experiences to researching and fact-checking information and the essential editing and proofreading process. I couldn't have asked for a better partner.

Special thanks to Tim Block, Steve Kress, Lauren Mandel, Ted Gilman, and Tom Tyning for reading these essays and providing feedback to ensure accuracy and clarity.

I feel very fortunate to work with Ed Flickinger, publisher of Grackle Books. I am truly thankful for his encouragement, support, and expertise.

Biographies

Craig Newberger

Author Craig Newberger served as the Lower School science coordinator at Germantown Academy in Pennsylvania for over three decades. Combining hands-on investigations with outdoor explorations, Craig nurtured a passion for science and nature in thousands of inquisitive minds. He led a variety of natural science trips for his students and their families, ranging from Costa Rica to Cape Cod. Craig's belief in immersing students in firsthand experiences led him to dedicate decades of summers in Maine, where he and his wife, Trudy, directed the National Audubon Society Youth Ecology Camp on Hog Island, founded and directed the Family Camp, and joined the instructional team for Audubon's camp for educators. Craig has also worked as a naturalist at the Cape Cod Museum of Natural History and directed an environmental education program connected with the Cape Cod National Seashore. Craig plays guitar and hammered dulcimer and is known for his sing-a-longs at assemblies and campfires. Craig is the author of *Spring Processional: Encounters with a Waking World* and *Summer Light: Encounters with a Vibrant World*.

Steve Morello

Steve Morello is an award-winning photographer, writer, and storyteller, known for telling a story with his images. Steve created the Little River Photo Workshops to share his skill and craft with others on his property in North Berwick, Maine. Steve is a National Geographic certified photo instructor and teaches for National Geographic and Lindblad Expeditions on expeditions around the planet. He is the author of *The Traveling Nature Photographer*.

Sherrie York

A self-taught printmaker and compulsive wanderer of landscapes, Sherrie York finds her inspiration in the natural world. A long-ago college fieldtrip to draw backyard chickens was the genesis of a career that has encompassed environmental education, natural history illustration, and fine art. Her illustration clients have included several national and international conservation organizations, and her fine art is included in corporate, private, and museum collections worldwide.

Ron Smith

Ron Smith teaches Environmental Science at Episcopal Academy in Pennsylvania, following twenty-five years of teaching for the Haddonfield School District in New Jersey. Along with faculty and staff from the Academy of Natural Sciences of Drexel University, Ron leads community science projects along the coast of New Jersey, with a focus on shorebirds and horseshoe crabs. He directs the Drexel University Environmental Science Leadership Academy and founded the Life Science Field Training Institute for Pinelands Preservation Alliance, a program that trains educators in field methods in community science. Ron is the author of *Adventures in Community Science*.

www.ingramcontent.com/pod-product-compliance
Lightning Source LLC
Chambersburg PA
CBHW052118030426
42335CB00025B/3047